THE HOMEOWNER'S GARDEN DESIGN GUIDEBOOK

A no-nonsense 3-step system to start designing and landscaping your dream garden

ISABELLA WOODS

In this list of gardening mistakes, you MUST avoid, you will learn:

- Thirteen of the most commonly made mistakes beginner gardeners make without realizing it.
- The secret to unlimited amounts of gardening knowledge. Without having to learn a damn thing!
- How to be part of our Facebook community filled with friendly and supportive gardeners.

Scan the QR code below with your mobile device to receive your **FREE BONUS GIFT!**
Or go to www.thegardenarchitectbooks.com.

Contents

Part III
Post-Design

Introduction

So, you want a garden that has YOU written all over it? A personalized design that a friend will see and say, "This is exactly you?" A place that fits your home, what you want in a garden, and how you envision your ideal outdoor space to be? like." Of course, they won't put it that way exactly, but you get the idea.

Maybe you just moved into a new home or want to take apart your old garden and erect a new one. On the other hand, perhaps you have a knack for gardening and want to help a friend renovate theirs. Whatever the case, let me assure you that you CAN create the dream garden you like! And guess what? You don't need to be an extraordinary visionary (let's leave that for the Bezos and Zuckerbergs) or even take an architecture class online to get started.

I get it. Your garden doesn't look how you want it to because of the environment. What about the bugs and insects destroying it? You're thinking, "How on earth will it be possible to deal with issues such as these?" Worse, you don't know much about designing or gardening, though you imagine having a beautiful one. Or, you might want to renovate the garden but don't know if you have the budget for it, knowing that it could cost thousands if you hire people to do it for you! And that's not the kind of expense you want to incur.

I will reiterate my previous statement. Despite these realistic concerns, you can still create the perfect garden design tailored to your needs and very budget-friendly.

Planning a garden design all by yourself, whether big or small, is complicated. I'm saying this because I'm not here to tell you lies or make up fantasies about it being easy. However, you can do it, as you are not alone. You now have the perfect guide by your side to help you from start to finish.

First, you have to understand what a good design is. Yes, you're probably already imagining what your picture-perfect garden design would look like; the relaxing area with the greyish cushions, etc. But creating a good garden design that you will fall in love with goes beyond simply the images you have in mind. The perfect garden is a space designed to take advantage of environmental elements now and in the future while at the same time looking unique to your standards. In simple terms, a good garden design must be functional and fit your needs.

The Homeowner's Garden Design Guidebook is a complete garden-owners'/homeowners' guide on designing your garden. I intend to take you through everything from garden styles to climate, garden goals, and much more. Then, after reading this book, you can go outside with your visualized ideas on paper and know exactly what to do to your outdoor space. All of the thought-out steps outlined in this book will give you that added advantage to creating that fantastic garden, steps that WILL transform your dreams into reality.

A quick story about how I got here:

You see, I became a bit obsessed with garden designs after recognizing that owning a garden went beyond simply growing veggies and other crops. I randomly renovated my garden from time to time because I wanted to try out new things. Basically, I couldn't keep to a design. Some were disasters, as I thought only about the aesthetic appeal over functionality, and some were better. Finally, I got the hang of it with time and didn't need to tear down my garden to erect a new design. Instead, I created a design that allows for changes over time, is functional, and fits my needs as well as my family's.

Luckily, I married someone who shared my obsession with garden design. We turned this hobby into a business. And now here I am, writing this book, understanding the complexities and misinformation involved in designing.

Because of my passion for gardening and helping people, I was compelled to create a book that clears up the confusion and difficulty within garden design. My dream is to be able to provide the opportunity for any homeowner (knowledgeable in gardening or not) who wants to create a beautiful garden.

This book is divided into three parts. Part 1 is on pre-garden design, where we discuss everything you need to know before we bring pen to paper. In part 2, called "Designing," you will discover how your ideal garden will look. And finally, part 3 goes over some great tips before you start physically landscaping.

I want to believe you are all in. So, why don't we get started with that?

PART I

Pre-Designing

WHAT YOU NEED TO KNOW
BEFORE WE START

Your Lifestyle Creates Your Garden

"My garden is my most beautiful masterpiece."

Claude Monet

In today's hyper-digitalized world, most of us live increasingly busy lifestyles without the spare time to step back and relax. Because of this harsh reality, our brains are constantly overloaded to the point where we become easily irritable and error-prone. Ultimately we completely burn out. However, we deserve much better!

You deserve to take a break and bask in a blissful haven occasionally. Gardening can be the perfect oasis you need to escape life's never-ending stress! It feeds your soul and lets your brain relax and release pent-up tension. I feel blessed when surrounded by the scent of fresh soil and an ever-growing display of plants.

But guess what is even better? Building a perfectly designed garden without having to spend your entire savings on hiring a professional designer! Most of us reading this book want to experience the intense satisfaction and fulfillment that comes with using your hands to creatively design and build a beautiful-looking garden where you and your loved ones can create new memories. Certainly, most of my fondest memories are with my family in our garden, especially the times when I had a long day and found my husband and kids having laid out a picnic in our garden (with our freshly grown fruits and vegetables) amongst the blossoming flowers. Fun experiences like these become a part of daily life when you have a beautiful garden you want to be in.

So, how do you design your own garden to serve as a beautiful masterpiece and a perfect oasis? It begins right at the planning phase. Just like the way you need a well-detailed blueprint to design a beautiful home, it's also important that you create the best design plan for your garden, no matter what the size of the space you have.

As beginners in gardening, most people tend to be misguided by unverified and inadequate information on garden design that they get via other people or online. I have experienced first-hand how misleading such information can be. As such, I understand where you're coming from. In this chapter, we'll do a simplified step-by-step analysis of the different factors that can influence how your garden will look at the end of your garden design project. You will discover that these elements are things that you have probably never considered to be of immense importance when you decide to set up your own garden.

But before we go into the details, I need you to understand that the journey of designing your garden is a very personal one. For many avid gardeners like myself, when we think of designing a garden, we think about the creation of a special place. Thus, as the owner and user of a garden, it is essential for you to have the most significant and final say in most, if not all, of the planning decisions. No matter how well-trained a professional garden designer will be, their choices cannot be as great as yours. Why? Pretty simple—you and your loved ones will be the ones using the garden the most. Nobody can do a better planning job than you, as you are the only one who knows what will work and what won't for you in particular. So say to yourself, "I've got this!"

At this point, you have your pen and paper out and ready to use! Now, let's explore the essential areas of your life that you must consider before designing your garden.

Your Lifestyle

Every aspect of your lifestyle and who you are is crucial to designing and creating your outdoor space. Personally, my husband loves to watch football games. But the best part of watching football games for him is having a tasty burger to enjoy as he watches. We can say that's a part of his lifestyle, right? This lifestyle is reflected in our garden design, as we have an area for barbequing. So every time before the football game begins, my husband grills the meat while I prepare the rest of the burger ingredients, then we both sit down to watch the game!

Here are some important lifestyle elements you must consider in designing your garden.

Family

Whether it's done on an acre of land or using a few pots on an urban balcony, gardening is an activity that enables you to share a sense of purpose with your loved ones. Hence, considering the needs of your family and friends must be a top priority when you're trying to come up with a perfect design for your garden.

Start by making a list of everyone likely to use the garden regularly. Your list has to be as detailed as possible. It should contain every member of your immediate family, along with extended family who will be regularly visiting, friends, and every other person special to you.

Having listed out the names, the next element to include is their ages and needs. For example, if you are a mother like myself who has younger kids, their age range will ultimately influence the size of garden space you will allot for playing. Perhaps you're thinking of adding water features like a pool or a fish pond to your garden. However, suppose your children are curious youngsters; in that case, you can easily incorporate more safety measures into your plans, such as fences and gates, so your children won't have the ability to fall in.

Besides young children, you may also have older parents, relatives, or family members, who might use wheelchairs or find it hard to walk long distances. Having full knowledge of their needs enables you to design a garden in a way that also gives them the chance to enjoy your garden. Considering your family in your garden design may also find that having a BBQ area is necessary!

The most important thing to understand here is that designing your garden should not only be about your lifestyle and preferences. Instead, a perfect garden is designed to satisfy the needs of everyone likely to use it and, most notably, to reinforce your family bond!

Maintenance Time

It is quite an accomplishment to design a beautiful garden. However, it is an entirely different thing to be able to maintain your garden well enough to make it flourish consistently.

Hence, you must ensure that you understand just how much time, money, and energy you will have and be ready to invest in your garden before you even start this project. You must be realistic and honest when figuring out the time you'll have to maintain the garden. To do this effectively, you have to consider the hours you spend at work and how much free time you will have to carry out routine garden maintenance activities like cutting the lawn, weeding, or watering.

Now, you might wonder, "What kind of connection exists between my garden design and my garden maintenance?" Well, the more design features you have in your garden (such as vegetable beds, for one example), the more maintenance will be required. So, for instance, if you want to plant fruit trees, you should ask yourself, "Will I have the time to deal with the huge amount of fruit those trees will produce when they are of fruit-bearing age?" If your answer is no, then you might consider using lower-maintenance trees in your garden. In the same way, you should consider how much money you are willing to spend on maintaining your garden.

Hobbies and Entertainment

Gardening serves as an excellent option for enjoying your hobbies. Therefore, you must design your garden in a way, so you get the chance to entertain yourself.

Take the time to figure out what you and your family love to do for fun. How exactly would you describe your social life? What activities excite you the most? For example, you might enjoy the stillness in your outdoor space for reading, painting, yoga, and sunbathing. Or perhaps you love socializing more often by having family dinners or barbecues. Whatever your hobbies or sources of entertainment are, you must ensure that you incorporate the necessary features for you to enjoy them into your garden design plan.

Pets

If you are someone who loves your pets as much as you love gardening, then you must take advantage of "petscaping." Ever heard of the word before? It's a relatively new concept that explains how your landscape and gardening design make special considerations for your pets.

As a pet owner, your garden must be designed to ensure your animal companions' safety while preventing them from causing any potential damage to your garden. Some design elements often utilized to build a pet-friendly garden include establishing boundaries and providing unique places for your pets to run and play.

What kind of pets you own and the total number will determine precisely which of these approaches you will utilize in your garden design. One mistake that many first-time gardeners tend to make is assuming petscaping only involves the task of choosing pet-friendly plants. On the contrary, it is more about designing your outdoor space in a way that you, your plants, and your animal companions will all be able to live and play safely without causing any interference to each other.

Storage

Creating adequate storage space is necessary for every gardener, whether your outdoor space is small or large. As a gardener, there is an awful lot you need to store, from gardening equipment to landscaping tools like your mower, hose, trowels, wheelbarrow, flowerpots, compost, seeds, gloves, etc. If you are a proud parent or pet owner, you may also need a storage space to keep backyard toys safe.

As you create your garden design, factor in your storage needs. There are different garden storage ideas—shelves, sheds, Potter benches—that you can use to store your gardening tools and materials properly. However, not all ideas will work for all gardens. As such, your primary job at the pre-designing stage is to estimate the number of garden tools you are likely to store. How exactly do you want to use your storage space? And what do you want it to hold? Of course, the size of your yard also plays a significant role in your garden storage choice.

In addition, it wouldn't be a bad idea to consider the effectiveness of that storage space as your garden grows in size and yield. Ask yourself, "Will this storage space still be the right fit in a few years?"

Privacy

It could be that your house is in a built-in area lacking outside space or that you have houses on either side of your home. Gardening in such an area would mean that being observed and overlooked as you go about gardening will be a daily reality. Perhaps you and your family may be very social people who don't care about who sees what, especially since your house will have a beautiful garden and deck. However, not everyone enjoys that experience! Some gardeners consider not having privacy to be a deal-breaker because they want their gardens to be their private sanctuary, one where they can be relaxed and free from prying eyes. In that case, you need to include the necessary measures to improve your garden's privacy in your design plan, which we will discuss in the coming chapters.

Your Wants and Needs

Having mapped out what your lifestyle constitutes and how it should influence your garden design, the next priority is to define your wants and needs. Understanding these two elements is crucial in making the best design decisions.

First, what are the differences between wants and needs? Your needs as a gardener refer to the necessary features your garden must have to ensure that it continues to flourish. You must have these features in your garden design plan! However, your wants as a gardener are extra features to enhance the functionality or beauty of your garden. You can do without them, but they are still important because your wants make your particular garden perfect for you. The table below will make it easier for you to understand the differences between wants and needs.

(Table 1 wants and needs in no particular order)

Wants	Needs
Front yard fountain	Vegetable bed
Hammock between 2 trees	Fencing for pets
Fire pit	Kids play area
Lounge area	Laundry drying space
Outside lights	Water storage

Sometimes it can be tricky to determine if a particular desire is a need or want. A simple way to solve that problem is always to ask yourself, "Will my garden suffer if I don't do this?" Here are some more tips you can utilize to figure out your wants and needs as a gardener.

Decide what is most important

The first logical thing to identify is your necessities. Since you already have a good idea of the different parts of your lifestyle that must be considered in your garden design, you can easily set your priorities while keeping those factors in mind. For example, at my house, we must have a gate, so our dog doesn't walk out into the street.

Take note of what you like and don't like

Now that you have sorted out the requirements that MUST be included in your garden features to make it flourish and be able to satisfy the needs of you and your family, you can proceed to your wants. A great way to start is to walk through your outdoor space and take note of what you like and don't like. The question that should be running through your mind is, "What do I like best and least about my home's surroundings as they currently exist?" Doing this gives you an idea of the current features you want to keep and the ones you want to let go or develop as you begin to design your garden.

Figure out what you want to see

Having discovered what you like and dislike about your outdoor space, it's time to think about the things you want to see and enjoy every time you walk into your garden or look out through your windows. For instance, if you decide you would love to see butterflies in your garden, then you may have to focus your garden design around a wildlife theme, where you will have plants that can easily attract butterflies.

Explore your interests

At this point, you already have a good idea of what you would love to see. So now the next task is for you to describe your landscape interests. Simply put, what do you see yourself doing in that garden? Is it spending a lot of time with plants or hosting dinner parties? Perhaps both?

Have an open discussion with your loved ones

One thing to note is that the task of defining your wants and needs does not have to be a one-person job. Discuss it with your family and close friends to help you make better decisions. Having such conversations keeps you from choosing just one focus for your garden. Instead, you better understand everyone's needs, enabling you to accurately divide your outdoor space to suit everyone's needs.

Start Your Gardening Notebook Now

You probably realize that everything we discussed in this chapter demands you do a little self-reflection to develop a more conscious awareness of your lifestyle, wants, and needs and how you can connect them to your garden design. For this reason, you need a gardening notebook, and today's the perfect day to start!

Recording in a notebook the new things you've discovered or may want to include in your design plan can be an enjoyable activity. Apart from this, a garden notebook allows you to reflect on your previous answers, beliefs, thoughts, etc. With this, you also understand who you were right from the starting point of your garden design project and how you evolved.

You might wonder if a notebook is really necessary, but think about how rapidly each day of your life passes. With a garden design notebook, you will be more enthusiastic about tracking your experiences. Besides, writing short points in a notebook helps you keep your thoughts organized, from which you can always seek help whenever the need arises. It will also come in handy as you use these notes later in the book.

It is, of course, preferred to have a separate notebook, but for those who don't have one lying around readily available, I have added a little notes section at the end of each chapter where you can write down some of the most important points.

Next up, we will discuss the other half of the planning stage, which focuses on the environmental elements in your outdoor space. Never forget that your garden is an extension of your home; therefore, your goal should be to transform that empty outdoor space into a little piece of paradise that will satisfy you, your family, and your friends.

Chapter Summary

- Building a perfectly designed garden is possible without spending your entire savings on hiring a professional garden designer!
- Every aspect of your lifestyle, especially your family, hobbies, pets, storage needs, and privacy desires, are essential factors to consider when deciding on the design of your outdoor space.
- Designing your garden should not only be about your own lifestyle and preferences. Instead, you should take into consideration the needs of everyone likely to use it.
- After mapping out how each lifestyle element would influence your garden design, identify and define your wants and needs.
- Enjoy the process of writing short points in a garden notebook, as it will help keep your thoughts in an organized form from your first step to your last in your garden design journey.

NOTES

2

Overcome Your Garden's Climate

"If you have never experienced the joy of accomplishing more than you can imagine, plant a garden."

Robert Brault

One unique thing I have discovered from my eight years of experience helping people create their most perfect garden designs is that the best garden layouts and designs invariably have certain features in common. Apart from being inviting and beautiful, these garden designs are usually easily accessible and well planned to suit both short and long environmental conditions.

Essentially, every garden is a function of its environment, which tends to change through the seasons. Therefore, failing to break down and understand each element that constitutes your outdoor environment before you begin designing can waste your efforts in the long run. For instance, if you fail to discover beforehand that your area experiences heavy rainfall, your entire garden gets waterlogged a few weeks after completing the design. I don't even want to imagine experiencing something like this.

Luckily for you, you don't have to worry about such consequences, as this chapter will provide an extensive and explicit explanation of how you can explore all the physical and environmental characteristics of your outdoor space before creating your design.

In the last chapter, we established the importance of having a garden design notebook to help you with this journey. Well, this is another perfect time that requires you to pull out your pen and paper! In most of this chapter, you will be required to do some research as you head out and do a tour of your garden. Therefore, it might take a while for you to achieve everything we're about to discuss. But, you have nothing to worry about because this stage of garden design planning is not complicated. In this chapter, we have broken down the entire research process into manageable steps that will enable you to do your tasks comfortably and at your own pace. So, let's go for it already!

Climate

Climate forms the basis and natural foundation on which all planning and designing decisions must be made. To ensure your garden design is a great success, you must familiarize yourself with the climatic characteristics of your outdoor space, including sunlight, rainfall, wind patterns, and soil types.

Sun Exposure

When incorporating environmental factors into your garden layout, it is always best to start by analyzing the amount of sunlight and shade available within your outdoor space.

Adequate sunlight is one of the most critical gardening elements if you want a garden with healthy and high-quality vegetables, fruits, or flowers.

To accurately determine the amount of sunlight your garden gets at different times, you must first understand that sunlight is a highly dynamic climate element, constantly moving throughout the day and from one season to another. So unlike what you might have assumed before, not every open area in your garden space receives a good amount of sunlight. As a result, the amount of sunlight your garden gets in the morning will differ from the afternoon and evening. The same thing applies to seasons: we have more sunlight in summer than during winter.

Apart from these natural factors, we also have certain human-influenced elements that affect the sunlight exposure your garden will likely get at different times of the day, including buildings, walls, trees, and more. For example, in the late fall, when the sun exposure is lower, having a tall tree or building next to your outdoor space could produce a large shaded area in your garden.

To find out this information about the sun and shade aspects of your garden, you should endeavor to visit your garden at different points during the day. Here is a formula that has offered me productive results as a garden designer over the last few years. First, you start taking note of the garden's sunlight exposure early in the morning, right after the sun rises. Then keep visiting every two hours to measure the amount of the garden's sunlight exposure and where shadows fall in the garden. If you don't have that luxury, check in three times a day—morning, midday, and evening.

Remember to take your pen, highlighter, and paper with you every visit. This is because as you observe, you will have to capture a picture of the garden's sunniest and most shady areas. An excellent way to do this is to make a simple sketch of your outdoor space, then color the sunnier places with a yellow highlighter and the shadier places with a pen or pencil. At the end of the day, you should have several sketches from your morning, afternoon, and evening visits.

Drawing is not required for you to get an idea of where the shadiest and sunniest parts of your garden are, however. You can simply write down in words where the sun is for each of your visits in a day to get the job done or take photos. Whatever result you get at the end of the day will help you understand what category your entire garden or its specific area falls into regarding its sunlight exposure. Here are the different types.

- **Full sun**: An area that gets at least 6 hours of direct sunlight throughout the day.
- **Partial Sun**: An area that gets between 3 and 5 hours of sunlight.
- **Partial Shade**: An area that gets 3 hours or less of sun exposure.
- **Dapple Sun**: A dappled sun garden is not shaded. Instead, the garden's sunlight exposure is filtered either through tall buildings, trees, bush branches, fences, slats, etc.

Generally, getting to know how much sunlight your outdoor space gets, and at which hours during the day it receives it, makes your job as a garden designer very easy, especially when it comes to selecting the best area for your planting activities as well as the choice of what plants to use in your garden. Every plant has a tag that helps you understand the plant's sun exposure requirements. So, for example, a plant that requires at least six hours of direct sunlight cannot survive in a shade garden.

Wind Patterns

Taking climate elements like wind flow patterns into account when planning your garden design can save you from a lot of capital damage in the future. Almost every area on earth is likely to experience high winds at one point or another. While it's possible that heavy rain may not cause a lot of damage when your garden is designed with well-detailed drainage, the arrival of a windstorm has a high chance of damaging a garden if no preparation is made to combat it.

To create a wind-proof strategy, you must determine how wind moves through your outdoor space. One thing to look out for is the layout of nearby buildings and paths around your garden area. In some cases, you might discover that these buildings have created a kind of wind tunnel in your garden. Another thing you can do is simply look at your garden on a windy day and notice which bushes, trees, and plants are moving the most. Also, don't forget to look at the ground; when the wind picks up, you will usually see dead leaves or things like plastic bags thrown around in a circular motion. Then note down which areas you have seen the most movement to know what areas to avoid or improve for in the future.

Strong wind may damage young smaller plants but not necessarily big ones. However, it could be that the area with the most wind is the best place to plant in terms of its soil quality and the amount of sunlight and rainfall it gets. Suppose you have discovered that there are windy areas that could cause harm to plants. In that case, you could begin to look for creative and effective windbreak options that you can incorporate into your garden design plan. These options vary in terms of simplicity. For example, there are cases where you simply have to create semi-permeable fencing. Similarly, you might have to go with other windbreak options like trellises or several taller plant structures to help disperse heavy wind pressure.

If you are new to the area you live in, you can always go the extra mile and ask questions to people who have been residents for a while. For example, they might be able to give information on periods when substantial winds tend to arise in the area.

None of us want to see our beautiful garden end up in disarray with blown-off leaves, broken stems, and soil loss after an intense windstorm. Conducting a little research on the wind flow pattern and incorporating it into the final decision of our garden design plan will ensure the protection of your blissful haven, no matter how intense and crazy the winds get.

Types of Soil

Like learning sun and wind patterns, getting to know your soil is vital to creating the perfect garden design! Soil testing is the best method to discover all the essential traits of your soil, including its nutrients, toxins, and carbon level.

The first thing to understand about exploring your soil type is that there are six main types of soil: chalky, clay, loamy, peaty, sandy, and silty. Each of these soil types has specific and unique characteristics. Therefore, testing your soil type is not just about looking at it. You need to feel it! The best way to feel the texture of your soil is to pick a small amount of it, then add very little water and try rolling it between your hands. As you roll, you have to observe keenly. Here are some features you can look for to identify different soil types.

- **Peaty:** As its name implies, peaty soil contains lots of peat. It is usually dark in color. When rolling it between your hands or squeezing it, you will most likely feel its spongy nature. It is rarely found in gardens.

- **Chalky:** You are most likely to find this particular soil type if your garden has an area with chalk or limestone bedrock. Chalky soil is quite stony. Due to its rocky texture, it tends to rapidly leach out certain mineral nutrients such as iron and manganese. An excellent way to improve its quality is to add compost and fertilizer regularly.
- **Clay:** When you add water to test clay soil, you will quickly feel its lumpy, slimy, sticky texture. Perhaps this explains why clay soil is the only type you can roll into a ball that will retain its shape. In addition, clay soil is very high in nutrients for soil that drains poorly and goes hard when dry.
- **Sandy:** Sandy soil has a very gritty texture. As such, if you manage to roll it into a ball, it will crumble apart easily. It is pretty easy to drain water from sandy soil because it dries out quickly. However, it tends to leach more nutrients during the rainy seasons. As such, you must provide added organic matter (compost) to retain its mineral content.
- **Silty:** When you find a soil type to be extremely smooth to the touch, there is a high possibility that you are holding silty soil. This soil type is made of the finest soil particles. Like clay soil, you can easily roll silty soil into a ball. However, it cannot maintain that shape. Though it is a free-draining soil type, silt soil can retain moisture and contain more nutrients than sandy soil.
- **Loamy:** This particular soil type is the most ideal for gardening, as it is not prone to waterlog, nor does it drain nutrients quickly. On the contrary, it is packed with nutrients. Since loamy soil is a mixture of clay, sand, and silt, you will discover that it has different-

sized soil particles as you roll the soil between your hands. As such, it can easily roll into a ball. However, it would not be able to maintain that shape.

As you determine the dominant soil type in your garden, always remember to write in your gardening notebook all the results you get. No matter the size of your outdoor space, you must ensure that you test the soil from different areas. So, the larger your outdoor space, the more places you have to explore.

When you can carry out this experiment effectively, you will discover that the soil type and quality can vary from one area to another. Such knowledge will guide you when creating your garden design and layout plan. For example, places with good soil quality will become the main planting areas, and areas with poorly-conditioned soil can be improved or reserved for other garden features like storage space, BBQ area, etc.

An adequate understanding of the dominant soil type in your garden through soil testing enables you to determine if that soil is ideal for gardening conditions. If the soil is not suitable, you can easily utilize different realistic ways to improve the soil, like using organic matter such as manure or home-grown compost or going to a local garden center where you can find pre-mixed fertile soil. Imagine what would happen if you had no idea what part of your outdoor space had good or poor soil quality. Without knowing, you could be growing plants that are destined to die quickly. Or you may place an external kid play center on an area packed with loamy soil, where you could have grown the most fruitful trees or beautiful and colorful flowers.

Rain

Rainwater is the best source for watering your garden. A general rule of thumb in gardening is that plants require at least one inch of rain per week for the continuous flourishing of the garden. This is in addition to the complementary efforts of other environmental factors that we have discussed earlier, including soil conditions, sun exposure, and wind patterns in that area.

Unlike the case of sunlight exposure, where you have to monitor the weather every two hours per day, you may only have to write down what the rain conditions are on a weekly or monthly basis. However, remember that these conditions change from season to season. For example, fall shows more rain, while summer has less. You can also search the internet to find the amount of rain you can expect in your area.

Every gardener prays only to get rainfall that will provide exactly enough water for their planting activities. However, our prayers may not always be answered due to the variations in seasons. We can neither control a natural element like rainfall nor avoid situations where water from the rain is too much or too little. However, certain features you can incorporate when creating your garden design will control these two disadvantageous situations.

- **Too much rain**: Firstly, it is essential to note that too much rain is relative to the climate. Heavy rain during intense sunlight and heat cannot be regarded as too much rain, given the other factors. That said, features a garden design can include to handle cases of too much rain include having a raised row garden setting, which undeniably helps easily handle issues of drought and excessive rain. Ensuring your garden has a free-draining soil type can also be very helpful.

Sand drains soil well. Perhaps try adding some to your soil if it becomes waterlogged frequently.

- **Not enough rain**: When you discover that the rain conditions in your area during dry seasons like summer tend to be very poor, you can incorporate certain water conservation features when creating your garden design plan to manage the water quantity. Some options include building cisterns to serve as large water storage options, installing a drip irrigation system, using water-saving containers as plant pots, or even investing in a sprinkler.

Animals and Insects

Whether your home is in an urban or rural location, your outdoor area will always be an ecosystem that attracts wildlife species, be it animals or insects. As such, you must verify the kind of animals or insects in abundance in your area. Some of them may be detrimental to the growth of your garden, while others may be beneficial.

To keep the balance between the good and bad insects/animals, you can use the structure and design of a garden to control the kind of wildlife species that will visit or make a home there. For example, you may discover that your immediate environment is one with a lot of deer. To protect your garden and ensure that these deer do not gain access, you could include features like sunken beds, terraces, higher borders, or sheer slopes.

On the other hand, you may also discover native birds in your area. Knowing how beneficial these birds could be in helping you reduce the number of insect pests in your garden, you could incorporate certain features to help entice them, like sacks of seed or a small birdhouse.

Enjoy the Process

And this is where we wrap things up for chapter 2! Quite a lot, isn't it? At this point, it would be perfectly normal for you to feel overwhelmed with a large amount of valuable information we've now covered. Nonetheless, this process can also be a gratifying experience. Imagine that moment when you are out in your garden with a cup of coffee just after sunrise. How peaceful would you feel? Even though, at that point, your goal may be only to observe how much sunlight exposure your garden gets in the morning, you tend to feel so relaxed that a lot of ideas come to your head. And the best place to save those ideas is your gardening notebook! You never know how valuable those ideas might be to the later stage of your design journey, so make sure to jot them all down. Enjoy the discovery process!

Chapter Summary

- Every garden is a function of its environment, so you must consider all the elements that constitute the overall environment of your outdoor space before you begin to design it.
- Analyze the sunlight and shade available within your outdoor space by visiting your garden at different points during the day.
- Find out how wind moves through your outdoor space by considering the layout of nearby buildings and trees or/and start asking around if people know anything about the wind conditions.
- Figure out your soil type by feeling the texture of your soil.
- Carry out some research on the rain conditions in your area by writing down/searching online about the frequency of rainfalls in the area on a weekly or monthly basis.
- Verify what kind of animals or insects are in abundance in your area. Some could be beneficial, and others could be detrimental to your plants.

NOTES

3

Transformative Garden Styles

"Gardens are the result of a collaboration between art and nature."

Penelope Hobhouse

In this book's first and second chapters, we focused on identifying and understanding the specific environmental factors and elements of your lifestyle that should influence your garden design. Our next point of action in this journey is to establish a garden style that best fits those factors.

You probably already had an idea of how you wanted your garden to look even before picking up this book. Perhaps in the past you saw pictures of fancy garden designs from your favorite lifestyle magazines or online tools like Pinterest and noticed that everything seems to be arranged in a rhythmic structure in each of those designs. So, how does the magic happen? It's simple; it all starts with a garden style.

A garden style is a tool that helps simplify your garden design by creating boundaries of what should go in it and what should not. At this point, if I asked every reader to list what they want to have in their dream garden, we could spend the whole day going on and on because we have so many ideas. While some of these ideas may be useful, others may not necessarily be consistent with the kind of goal you want to achieve in your particular garden. That is precisely why you need a specific garden style you can keep in mind. In a way, it helps you focus your mind, efforts, and buying impulses on only the key components that will work well together for your garden design. Without an integrated garden style, your garden could become a messy disarray of visual loudness.

You do not have to be an expert garden designer to determine your best garden style. As we established in Chapter One, garden designing is a personal journey, and you have what it takes to be successful at it. Besides, it could also be those ideas you had about your dream garden that already fit into a particular style. But you will never know if you don't keep reading! So, let's get started!

Hardscaping vs. Softscaping

Before we explore the different types of garden styles, it is crucial that you first understand the various components that constitute a garden style, categorized into two main parts: hardscaping and softscaping features.

Hardscaping features generally refer to the physical, non-living, and permanent elements that form the outline of your garden. They include everything in your outdoor space that is made of stone, brick, concrete, wood, metal, etc. So your pathways, walls, fences, wood installations, lighting, etc., are all part of hardscaping elements. Softscaping elements, on the other hand, are the living part of your garden landscape. They include ornamentals, shrubs, trees, lawns, hedges, etc.

Each of the garden styles we are about to discuss has a unique combination of hardscaping and softscaping elements for your outdoor space. Let's explore them in detail.

Garden Styles

Formal Garden

Formal-style gardens rely on a rigid hardscaping and softscaping design arrangement. Everything in a formal garden is planned and laid out in a straight, narrow, and symmetrical pattern. The same elements are typically placed on either side of an axis to achieve proportional balance. So, for instance, if you have a particular flower planted on the right-hand side of your garden walkway, there must also be a similar flower planted on the opposite side.

Apart from the perfect symmetry of geometrical forms, formal garden styles are also characterized by flower beds, borders, and shrubbery arranged in geometrically designed beds, trimmed formal hedges, edges, cypress, Ashoka trees, and topiary. If you want to see one of the most popular formal gardens in the world, I recommend looking up the Gardens of Versailles in France.

If you're looking for some visual support to match the image by these garden styles then scan the QR code below to see what the next garden styles look like.

Modern Garden

The modern garden style is formal and focuses more on the heavy use of materials like metal and concrete rather than nature. This style incorporates hardscaping elements like geometrical stepping stones and architectural sculptures made from concrete, resin, or ceramic. It also includes water features like ponds and fountains with clean lines and geometric shapes. A large, sleek garden planter is a must-have in modern gardens.

Modern garden styles often use trees with canopies that are not too large. However, these trees are primarily arranged in a row to create a hedge effect.

Minimalist Garden

As the name implies, a minimalist garden style uses a limited number of design elements. As a result, it is an excellent garden style for busy young people.

It involves using materials like rocks, gravel, and paving stones that require low or no maintenance. Minimalist gardens use container planters to grow interesting, attractive drought-tolerant plants that help add color and form to your garden. This garden style also relies on the building of rock or brick fences, walls, and borders to delineate the separate areas of your yard. Minimalist and modern gardens go hand in hand a lot of the time.

Traditional Garden

As a garden designer, if you are more concerned about balance and symmetry in your garden, you might consider this particular style. The traditional garden style is usually characterized by formal and architectural solid features like cleanly edged walkways, stone fountains, etc. Traditional gardens are usually dominated by vast expanses of perfectly trimmed green lawns and rows of formal hedges. Another distinct feature of the traditional gardens is that they are not always filled with bright and diverse colors. Most gardens that are designed using the traditional garden style tend to use only white as their accent color.

Informal Garden

Away from the world of formal garden styles with strict rules of design symmetry is a more open land of diverse styles known as informal garden styles. Informal garden styles are characterized by flowing curves and asymmetrical arrangements of garden features. Here, plants and ornamentals are planted informally and allowed to grow into their natural shapes. Unlike formal garden styles, this particular set of garden styles takes great delight in using a mix of exciting colors while still giving off a natural garden look.

Regarding hardscaping structures, informal gardens feature diagonal or curved pathways, native mixed hedging, natural-looking ponds, pools, etc. They also include tall shrubs and taller trees, which add to their vertical dimensions and help hide the garden area's edges to create a relaxed feeling.

Suppose you are more interested in allowing nature to find its ways rather than controlling the different elements in your garden. In that case, you will indeed find the informal garden styles very appealing. Studies have shown that informal garden styles are quite common, especially among beginners in the gardening game. Perhaps this popular preference for informal garden styles can be attributed to its relaxed yet intriguing design process.

Nonetheless, you must be careful with the informal garden styles. The fact that they are ruled by a more open and flexible design system could easily make you attempt a lazy approach which could, in turn, lead you to create a loose, uninspired, and limp garden design. Thus, you must always ensure that your purpose and intentions guide you.

Cottage Garden

The cottage garden style can easily be described as the relaxed and unruly version of the traditional garden style. Though the design layout for the cottage garden style has the same straight lines and geometric shapes as the traditional style, plants in the cottage garden are allowed to spill over the lawns and paths to create softer edges.

The cottage garden style also features colorful and diverse collections of mixed flowers, plants, edibles, and herbs. With this style, you can use any available garden space for planting. Generally, a garden designed in cottage-style projects gives the feeling of relaxation and somewhat an "organized mess."

Japanese Garden

The Japanese garden style is more subdued and minimalistic. The main goal of this style is to make your garden a place with little to no distraction where your mind can easily relax into a meditative state. It features mostly green moss, grass, or shrubs trimmed neatly into domes. Moss is essential as it signifies harmony, age, and tradition. Another unique feature of this style is sand raked into perfect line patterns to represent rivers and stones to represent mountains. Basically, the Japanese style enables you to incorporate minimal features in your garden while still giving it a natural and charming look.

Mediterranean Garden

This garden style originated from the countryside of many Mediterranean-facing countries, including France, Greece, Spain, and Italy. It features interesting landscape elements like pebbled or cobbled walkways, intricately patterned tiles, and rows of trim-clipped hedges or topiary. Another underlying element common with Mediterranean-style gardens is the erection of water features for cooling, especially during the hot summer.

In terms of softscaping elements, the plants and ornamentals used in this garden style usually have very bright and eye-catching colors. In addition, drought-tolerant plants like succulents, agave, or euphorbia, as well as strongly scented herbs like lavender and sage, are usually informally planted in Mediterranean-style gardens.

Woodland Garden

The woodland garden style is slightly different from the other typical garden styles in that it works best for heavily shaded garden areas. For example, suppose your outdoor space is located near the edge of a wooded area and surrounded by tall trees. In that case, you can easily utilize the woodland style to create the perfect garden design.

The pathways in a woodland garden are usually made with natural materials like mulch, gravel, stepping stones, or a boardwalk of pallet wood. An area of the heavily shaded space is typically cleared to create a walkway and reduce summer heat. The lower branches of the trees may also be trimmed to raise the canopy and enable some dappled light.

In most cases, only plants that require a level of shade tolerance thrive well in a woodland-style garden. The woodland garden style employs a mix of exciting and diverse textures, forms, and wood colors for its overall design.

Wildlife Garden

Wildlife gardens are one of the more recently developed styles. Like informal garden styles, the wildlife garden style goes against all forms of formalism. The only rule here is to design your garden nature-friendly and yet beautiful.

Let's start with softscaping elements. This unruly, naturalistic style is based on the concept of naturalizing plants in shrubberies. In simpler terms, it means allowing your plants to grow in their natural shapes and making the garden friendly for all animals, birds, and insects. The passages to your garden are also usually opened. Using the wildlife garden design allows nature and bulbous plants to grow unmoved and scattered in the grass, thus giving your wild garden scenery. In wildlife gardens, ornamental trees and shrubs are planted in forest flora. You may be surprised to know that many of the most beautiful hardy flowers thrive much better in rough places than they ever did in the old-fashioned beds. All in all, the wildlife garden style provides your garden with an attractive blend of beauty and adequate ecological utility.

Apart from the basic types of garden styles we just identified, there are also popular ones defined less by their layout and more by the plant and climate conditions that go with them. They include coastal, tropical, desert, and courtyard garden styles.

Coastal Garden

If your home is close to the seaside, you may want to design your garden using this style. Also known as the seaside garden style, it incorporates hardscaping elements such as stone walls, teak wood fences, and other strong structures to withstand high winds and seawater. In many cases, the coastal garden style tends to have a rather wild and fun theme for decorations. Some decor elements include lobster traps, flamingo statues, egrets or seagulls, etc.

Only a select number of tough native plants capable of withstanding the wind and salt air can thrive in coastal gardens. However, depending on the climate condition in your immediate environment, palm trees are, of course, well-suited for providing a coastal vibe.

Tropical Garden

The tropical style is best for gardens that are located in areas with warm, moist climates. Landscape elements such as simple dirt pathways, smooth pebbles, natural colored wood chips, crushed stones or gravel, etc., make up the hardscaping features of a tropical-style garden. In addition, the style includes colorful plants, exciting pottery collections, ponds with brightly colored fishes, or even a waterfall in your garden to liven up the space. A tropical-style garden usually contains plants with huge leaves and other jungle-like features, giving the garden its typical dense look.

Desert Garden

A desert or xeriscape-style garden is a garden with water-conscious features that helps ensure that your garden utilizes little or no irrigation. Nevertheless, the fact that this garden style is focused on being water-conscious doesn't mean that it cannot be beautiful.

A desert garden style utilizes permeable gravel ground covers, such as pea gravel and decomposed granite. Boulders may also be added to round out the space. In addition, the desert style includes a mix of native or no-fuss plants such as cactus, agave, and succulents, which will thrive in your garden with little human intervention. This particular set of plants tends to add to the beauty and intrigue of the garden.

One benefit of designing your garden in a desert style is that it requires very low maintenance, which is excellent, especially if you are someone who does not have much time to dedicate to regular maintenance.

City and Courtyard Garden

This particular garden style is especially great for city dwellers with smaller garden spaces. Using the courtyard garden style involves making the best use of a small space.

Elements of a courtyard garden include a fireplace or patio heater to make the garden more comfortable during winter, lighting to make it visible at night, a dining or relaxation area, and decorative planting containers that add style to the space. The vertical space of the courtyard can also be used to grow vines or to display ornamental plants.

One thing you must understand about the garden styles we have discussed so far is that you do not have to be constrained by a particular style. We all have different unique tastes. As such, you can use your creativity to combine as many garden styles as your imagination inspires efficiently. In my opinion, what is most important is for you to understand how each garden style works. It gives you more chances to exercise your creativity!

Creating a Garden Mood Board

Deciding on the right garden style can be overwhelming, especially for beginners. From my personal experience of helping others create their perfect garden design, I have come to realize that one of the best methods to come up with a clear direction for your ideal garden style is not only to identify the things you like and do not like but also to be able to picture them collectively. Having them in a collective place helps you easily visualize the common thread that runs through your thoughts. This, in turn, enables you to get a clearer picture of the garden styles that best suit you! Doing all of these alone can be quite hard, which is why you need a garden design mood board to make your job easy.

Before we go into details about what a garden design mood board is and how it works, I need you to understand that making a garden mood board is not obligatory. Some of you may be too busy to make one or feel like you don't need to make one since you already have a clear idea of the specific garden styles you want to incorporate in your garden design.

Now that we have gotten that out of the way let's focus on what a mood board is and how it can be helpful to your overall garden design plan. A garden mood board is a well-arranged collage of pictures, materials, pieces of text, etc. It is a visual tool that helps you efficiently convey or project a particular style, concept, or "mood" for your garden design. Not only does a garden mood board help you think of ideas for your project, but its creation process is a lot of fun.

A garden mood board can be created in two forms, either digital or paper. A digital garden mood board involves using online tools like Pinterest and Canvas to create collages of pictures. A paper-based garden mood board uses scissors and glue to fix images to a piece of cardboard or an artist's canvas, if available.

To make the activity very easy and fun, we have identified three basic steps that you can take to create a simple and efficient garden mood board.

Collect

The first step in creating a garden mood board is to collect images or visuals of everything that interests and inspires you. This could include photos of backyards, plants, furniture, textures, materials, etc. Remember we said there are two options for creating a garden mood design? You could decide to use the old-fashioned style of clipping pictures from magazines. You could also take photos of specific areas that spark your interest or search for images online. However, it would be best if you did not forget that some of your best ideas may be from beyond the screen.

Another thing to note in this collection stage is that you are free to save as many images as you like. You could create different collections for different structures to make things more organized. For example, you could have a specific furniture collection, pools, plants, etc.

Curate

Now that you have successfully gathered enough inspiration, it's time to refine your collection only to accommodate the most important ideas. This elimination process requires comparing images and identifying the common elements you like the most. You could even go the extra mile to describe what you want in your garden notebook.

Nevertheless, you must be very selective at this stage. You can cut down the pictures to only two to three for your ideal version of each collection. Suppose you are using online tools like Canvas or Pinterest. In that case, it is highly recommended that you create a different ideabook or board where you can save only your selected favorites.

Arrange

Having selected a handful of images from the dozens you had before, the last step is putting the finishing touches on your garden mood board. This stage involves the arrangement of your picture collage in a way that captures your landscaping vision.

Apart from visualizing your vision, having a visual representation of your ideal garden makes it much easier for you to share your ideas with others. You could even share the fun by including them in the activity of making a mood board with you. Or you could give them the chance to create their own separate mood board so that you can see what they want in the garden.

In my experience as a garden designer, I have worked with couples who had differing design ideas for their garden but did not communicate. It turned out to be a massive problem as their final garden design did not express the vision that they had in mind for that project. Thus, it would help if you incorporated your desired design idea into your garden design plan.

Chapter Summary

- A specific garden style helps you simplify your garden design by creating boundaries of what should go in it and what should not.
- Your garden landscape is made up of hardscaping (physical) and softscaping (living) elements.
- All garden designs fall under two basic types, formal and informal.
- Strict rules of design symmetry characterize formal garden styles. In contrast, informal garden styles have more relaxed and diverse rules with a mix of exciting colors.
- Creating a garden mood board that constitutes a well-arranged collage of pictures, materials, and pieces of text makes it easier for you to decide the "right" garden style.
- The three steps to creating a perfect mood board involve collecting everything that interests you, curating them to accommodate only the most important ones, and arranging them on a single board.

NOTES

PART II

The Secrets to Designing!

4

How to Accomplish all Your Garden Goals

As in all of the arts, the best garden designers take risks. Only by taking risks can you come up with something exciting and original.

James Van Sweden

In the last three chapters, we successfully covered the fundamental subjects you must understand before beginning your garden design. Thus, I am pleased to inform you that we are ready to dive into the design stage. Applying everything we learned in the preceding chapters begins right here.

The first stage of your garden design adventure focuses on goal-setting. I believe this stage is the most personal of the entire garden design process, as each person tends to have a unique reason for wanting a garden. Therefore, I would like to share my story to show you how personal goal-setting can be to you and your garden.

My journey into the world of gardening and garden design was entirely unplanned. In fact, younger me never saw myself doing anything related to it. One fateful day, this changed when my son walked out into our garden without me noticing.

At that time, my baby boy was learning how to walk, so he was always grabbing onto everything he could find.

I heard a big *bang*, followed by the loud cries of my son. I ran out into the garden as fast as my legs could carry me, and right there on the ground was my son lying next to a plant pot that had fallen off a small bench. I had never felt so scared in my life. I thought of so many scary what-ifs: What if the plant pot had landed on top of him? What if I had been too far away to hear the noise quickly? What if the injury had been worse?

For me, this particular accident opened my eyes to the fact that I needed to take practical actions concerning the design of my garden. That very night when my husband came home from work, I begged him to teach me about garden design, which happened to be his main field of study in college. Of course, I could not learn much about the subject in just one night. However, that day, I promised myself I would learn as much as possible about all I needed to know to create and design the perfect garden for my family. That one night of garden design gave birth to a special routine of many more night classes, as my husband and I spent time discussing and visualizing different ideas we could do to design our garden. To this day, the nightly talks we have about gardening have not stopped.

I kept acquiring as much garden design knowledge as possible. Eventually, after about six months, I finally felt confident enough to apply all the skills I had learned. I drew out my goals, and with help from my family, I completely designed a whole new garden within three months. First, it took me 30 days to sketch my reality on paper with much trial and error, then another two months to bring this reality to life. At that point, I was overwhelmed with an incredible feeling of happiness and fulfillment. I mean, who wouldn't? Now I was able to fulfill my duty as a super-mother by creating and designing a garden where my sons could play safely and where we could all enjoy ourselves as a family. This was almost eight years ago. For the best part of the last seven years, I have been helping people create their own perfect garden which embodies every aspect of their imagination. It has been amazing so far!

Like me, I know you also have a unique story to tell about the reason behind your desire to create the perfect garden design. Thus, your design goals should originate from your stories and the reasons embedded in them! For instance, you can easily guess from my story that one of my essential garden design goals was to build a safe play area for my sons and an outdoor dining space for family and friends.

Essentially, the process of setting goals for your garden design requires that you write down every single one of them inspired by your story. So what exactly is the point? Well, we'll discuss the exact reasons later in this book; but for now, you must understand that writing down your goals makes you more precise about what you want to achieve with your garden design. In addition, it gives you a clear picture of the destination you want to reach. Most importantly, when you approach your garden design process with clearly stated goals, you become far more likely to make effective and correct decisions to ensure the fulfillment of those goals.

At this point, I hope your paper and pens are ready to be utilized because, with the knowledge from this chapter and those simple tools, you will begin to write the success story of your garden design!

Setting Garden Design Goals

We have already established that goal setting is a personal task for everyone. Thus, our concern in this chapter is not to dictate to you the specific types of goals to set for your garden design. Instead, the main focus is to help you understand the practical art of setting goals. How do you set your goals in a way so that most, if not all, end up accomplished?

Beginners in gardening, experienced gardeners, and even professional garden designers, are unaware of how to do this. So, many tend to discover that the same goals reappear on their to-do list every new season. These recurring goals come from several simple things people tend to overlook. In a way, we cannot be blamed, because most online materials only provide a brief overview of goal setting.

Here is an example of what a typical garden goal list might look like. I will need:

- Focal point
- Patio
- Fire pit
- Scaling privacy
- Edible garden
- Outdoor dining space
- A "fifth room"
- Lounge area
- Pet-friendly space
- Toddler zone
- Living walls
- Permeable landscape
- Outdoor living
- Drought-tolerant native trees
- Backyard oasis

Many inexperienced gardeners tend to stop the goal-setting process at this point and immediately move forward to start implementing. But, unbeknownst to them, this is where the goal-setting process begins. If you want an ideal goal plan that can set up your garden for success, then it has to contain enough details to answer questions like, "Why is this goal important? How long will it take to complete this goal? Who will benefit from it?" and so on.

So how do we create a correct goal list? Well, our solution lies in our ability to understand and effectively apply the rules of the SMR formula.

The SMR Formula

The SMR formula is a practical guide for goal setting in garden design. The tool incorporates three essential criteria that can help you remain focused and increase your chances of accomplishing your goals. The S stands for "specific," the M stands for "measurable," and the R stands for "realistic." Now, let's examine why we would use these three criteria to improve our chance of completing our goals.

Specific

Every goal you write out for your garden design must be extremely specific. In this case, being specific involves clearly defining and stating your goals. Unfortunately, we often assume we have a good understanding of what we want to accomplish. As such, we comfortably write down our goals in very vague forms. Eventually, it ends up creating problems in the long run, as even you would be unable to explain what those 'vaguely defined' goals properly involve.

There are three simple steps to ensure that your garden design goals are specific. The first step is to identify the exact goal you want to achieve. Then you state why that particular goal is important to you and worthy of your time, effort, and resources. Finally, you might also need to identify the parties involved, for example, your spouse, family, or friends.

For example, here is what a vague goal might look like: "I want a fire pit in my garden." However, a more specific goal would be, "I want to build a fire pit in the right corner of my garden so that it will serve as the perfect outdoor gathering spot where I can relax with family, friends, and neighbors." For someone who lives in a cold area, a specific goal might be, "I want to build a fire pit so that I can enjoy the heat it provides even when I am relaxing outside."

From these examples, you can see that though we are referring to the same goal, the importance of the goal is portrayed differently. However, you would not have been able to tell the different inspiring factors behind the goal if they had been written vaguely.

In addition, clearly outlining your goals and backing them up with a strong "why" in terms of their significance to you gives you a clear direction and the motivating incentive to continuously work toward its accomplishment. So, you see, completing the simple task of specifying your goals comes with a 2-in-1 bonus package as your reward.

Besides, you will notice from the example we used that specifying your goals makes them sound more exciting and pleasing to the ears. It makes you think, "Oh, I can't wait to see this goal accomplished."

Measurable

Once you have clearly defined your goal, the second rule of the SMR formula is that you make your garden design goals measurable. It involves defining your garden design goals in a way that enables you to determine your progress and to know if you are on the right track to reach your goal and when you've accomplished it. For example, you might say to yourself, "I want more color in my garden." Firstly, this goal is not specific. Secondly, how do you know if you've accomplished your goal?

"I want more flowers in my garden" is more specific, but when will "more" be accomplished? When you've planted three flowers or 19? All of this confusion is avoided by making your goal measurable: "I want four differently colored flowers next to the pine tree, so when I look out of my kitchen window, my garden looks more colorful." A lot better, right?

To make your garden design goals measurable, ask yourself:

- How many?
- How much?
- How long?
- How do I know if I have accomplished my goal?

As a seasoned garden designer, I have discovered from my personal experiences and those I have helped that one effective way to get the best results is to keep good records. By making your goals measurable, you specify the progress indicators, and evaluating your efforts with these indicators keeps you accountable. Plus, it reinforces your focus on your goals. For instance, if you have planted orange and red flowers next to your pine tree, you'll know that planting two differently colored flowers would complete your goal.

Realistic

Having defined your goal specifically and made it measurable, your final task, according to the SMR formula, is to assess if the goals listed are realistic. A realistic goal is one for which you have the resources, time, and physical capability to accomplish efficiently. Assessing whether your goal is realistic or not is one of the most effective ways to ensure that you do not set yourself up for failure in the long run.

To show you why this realism is necessary, let's look at a different goal that has not applied much realism. My good friend, Emily's dream, was to have a wooden gazebo in the middle of her garden. The goal itself isn't unrealistic, but she only had a $500 budget, and gazebos usually start at $1,000 and just go up from there. To meet her budget goal, she would have to construct one herself, which is difficult since she is a busy teacher with little time throughout the week. Ultimately, she became disappointed in herself because she believed it to be a good goal she was simply failing at when it was not a good goal, to begin with.

Before jumping the gun and thinking your goals are ready to try, take a second look at them and ask yourself, "Is this goal realistic?" By asking yourself this simple question, your mind will be forced to find answers to why it is or isn't a realistic goal. If you find out that perhaps your goal has some problems, try to find a way to make it more practical and reasonable. For example, to make Emily's dream gazebo come true, she could increase her budget or perhaps wait for summer break to try and build it herself. This realization saves you from the heartache of throwing a good amount of resources and time into something that was set to fail right from the beginning.

Goal Setting Guide

I understand that sometimes it can be tough to incorporate the lessons we learn from a book into our daily lives. But you do not have to worry because, as I promised in the introduction of this book, I will walk through every step of this journey with you. Below, I have designed a guide that showcases what the outcome of a realistic goal-setting activity should look like.

	Specific	Measurable	Realistic
Focal point	When I walk into the garden from my backdoor, I want to see a focal point in the middle that will catch anyone's eye. It will be a small statue of some kind with a pathway leading to it from my backdoor.	I'll know I'm done when there's a clear pathway from my backdoor to the middle of my garden, where a small statue will be set up. No higher than 3 feet and no wider than 2 feet.	The pathway will be cost-efficient since it will be made of leftover stones sunk into the ground. I have found a small statue online for about $150 in my budget. None of this will require additional help.
Fire pit	In the back right of my garden, I would like a metal bowl with legs that will serve as a fire pit around a seating area.	Very easy to tell its progress, as it looks more and more like the gathering space it's designed to be. Easy to see if the fire pit is working or not.	If building it yourself with a smart plan and some scrap items, it should be accomplishable for less than $50.
Toddler zone	In the far left corner of the garden, a 13-by-13-foot patch of fenced-off grass for my kids to play in.	With the only construction needed being a 3-foot-high wooden fence, it will be easy to measure how close we are to finished.	The far back corner of my garden already has soft grass and only needs to be fenced off, which I can get my husband to do this weekend.

Now, compare this with the previously listed goals. You see that the SMR formula provides a layout to explore your goal, making it look more realistic and easily implemented. So write down those goals using the SMR formula, and let's go! For every goal you put down, I want you to consider how capable you are and how you can effectively leverage your skills and the knowledge you are amassing to achieve those goals to the fullest!

Having written down your specific, measurable and realistic goals, the next pertinent question is what to do with them. In the following chapters, you will discover the best ways to incorporate the goals you have written down into your garden design.

Chapter Summary

• Setting your design goals is the most personal task in this journey because your stories and their reasons should inspire these goals!

• Approaching your garden design process with clearly stated goals increases your chances of making effective decisions that will ensure achieving those goals.

• The SMR formula is a practical goal-setting guide that offers three essential criteria to help you define your goal more appropriately.

○ S represents "Specific," which involves clearly defining your goals by stating why you want the goal and those who will be involved in the goal.

○ M represents "Measurable," which involves defining your garden design goals to enable you to determine your progress using indicators.

○ R represents "Realistic," which involves assessing if you have enough resources, time, and physical capability to accomplish the goals you have clearly defined.

NOTES

5

Your First Design

Gardens are not made by singing, 'Oh, how beautiful,' and sitting in the shade.

Rudyard Kipling

Having identified their garden design goals, many beginner gardeners often make the mistake of going straight ahead to acquire building materials, ornamental plants, and other essentials to design their gardens. I understand that you might also be tempted to make the same mistake. I've been there, too. As such, I am well aware that successfully stating your goals on paper, especially using the SMR formula, will intensify the fire and zeal within you to transform those dreams from paper to reality.

Nonetheless, I must tell you that perfect gardens are designed not just by clearly identifying your goals and putting them on paper using the SMR formula; it further demands that you carefully observe your outdoor space and make a detailed plan for the picture of your garden you have in mind. Placing an item in your garden haphazardly without a plan can make the whole place look cluttered and unorganized, leaving your goals unachieved.

So how to ensure that such tragedy doesn't occur? Simple—with an accurate site survey of your outdoor space. Now, I bet you might not have heard of a site survey before, so let me explain. Site survey is a detailed measurement of your garden site and its different features. Think of it as similar to the blueprint of a house. Site survey is a drawn above view of your garden an house like you would see it on google maps. Having an accurate site survey is crucial to the success of your garden design and, eventually, your finished garden. So for this chapter, you and I will walk through the steps involved in creating an accurate site survey.

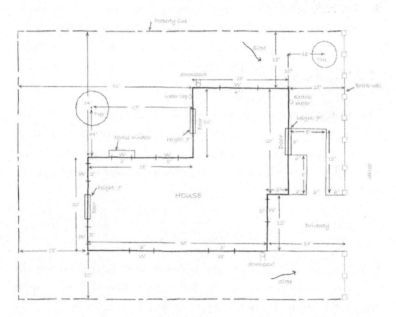

Typical site survey

Now I can understand that seeing this sketch might be a tad bit scary since it looks pretty detailed. Not to worry its actually quite simple. But first, you might already have a site survey of your house and outdoor space in your mortgage documents. Therefore, you should look there first. In that case, your goal in this chapter is to understand the best methods to recreate it in a simplified version. In the same way, we will also explore the necessary steps you need to take to create a site survey plan from scratch. Trust me, the activities lined up for this part are pretty fun and enlightening!

Why is creating a site survey important? Well, I'm sure none of us would want to put time and effort into creating a design only to find out at the time of building that your ideas would not fit into the size and shape of your outdoor space. Ouch! This's why you must have an overhead view of your garden and house with the correct measurements. The good news is that by creating an accurate site survey, you automatically become aware of each element's location, measurements and boundary lines. That information becomes your guardian angel, as it quickly helps you identify what will and won't fit your garden.

The practical concepts you will be learning in this chapter involve activities you might have to do over a few days. However, you do not have to be worried about the time frame, as it only means you are getting closer to your dream garden. So let's start!

Design Tools

The core process of creating a sketch plan and accurate site survey does not require fancy design tools like designing apps, drawing boards, French curves, or even computers. Instead, you are all set to do a great job with the simple tools we are about to identify and your drawing ability. Now, I know what some of you might be thinking: "Oh no! I can't draw!" Take a deep breath and relax because your drawing skills only need to be as good as an eight-year-old. Here are all the tools you will need:

- Pencil
- Eraser
- Paper/graph paper
- Ruler
- Colored pens or pencils
- Highlighters
- Tracing paper (optional)

Creating A Site Survey without A Sketch Plan

A sketch plan is a rough sketch showing the elements in your outdoor space. However, the site survey also provides detailed measurements of these elements within your outdoor space. As you probably have noticed, the only difference between these two sketches is measurements and accuracy. See Figure 1 below for an example of an official site survey.

Some of you reading this might already have a found your site survey. As I stated before, you will most likely find a site survey in your mortgage documents.

However, this tends to be quite detailed, and the fact is that we don't need everything included in one, just the simple features like fences, windows, doors, property lines, etc.

So how do we change this into a simplified site survey? First, you can place tracing paper over the site survey if you already have one, then trace over the hard outside lines of the house and the boundaries of your outdoor space. If you do not have tracing paper, you can redraw what you have on your site survey onto another piece of paper, simply using your eyes as a rough guide.

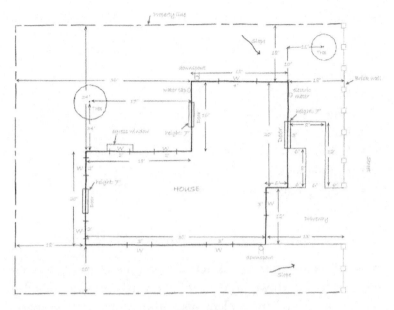

Figure 1: Typical site survey

Creating your Sketch Plan

What if you don't have a site survey? This is where a sketch plan comes in to save the day! A sketch plan is a rough drawing of your outdoor space that does not require any specific measurements or dimensions. In short, your sketch plan should be the drawing you look at to answer the question, "What key elements do I have in my garden right now?"

Surely you will notice that I emphasized the word "rough" when describing what a sketch plan is. It is a stepping stone to eventually making a better, neater, and more finalized drawing for your site survey, which will contain the accurate measurements of each part. The only difference between the sketch plan and site survey is that the site survey has measurements and is drawn to scale. So don't stress about accuracy at this point; remember, an eight-year-old child can do this, and so can you.

To make this section more practical, fun, and easy to understand, I have designed a simple sketch plan that will serve as our sample guide. Here it is below, followed by a more detailed look at each of its elements.

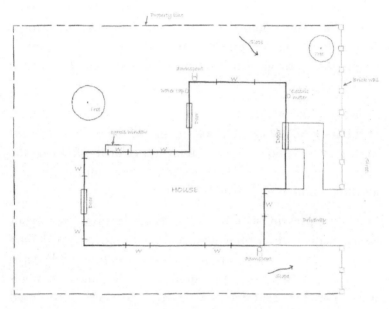

Figure 2: Typical sketch plan

Property Boundaries

The border lines surrounding the center's primary shape are the first thing you will most likely notice on that sample sketch plan. These borders represent your property lines.

House

Moving on from drawing our boundaries, we can concentrate on the house. Simply sketch out the shape of your home, just as in the sample sketch. Now, we all know that there are quite a lot of features in a house. So to make things easier, let's break them down.

Windows and Doors

Sketching out all the windows and doors in your house is essential. This is necessary because when designing your garden, the way it looks from the inside is just as important as how it looks on the outside. And, of course, you want to ensure that your garden is designed so that you can access it by using a particular door.

Looking at the sample sketch plan, you will notice that a door at the back of the house leads straight to the driveway. Apart from that, we also have two other entries at the front of the house. The house has about eight windows, indicating each location on the sample plan.

You can represent the different parts of the property in your sketch plans with symbols that make sense to you; it doesn't matter if these symbols are not "industry standard." What is most important is that you mark out what those symbols stand for. For example, in the sample sketch, we used rectangles to represent the areas of the house where the doors are, but with the label "D" right beside them as a means of recognition.

Downspouts and Water Taps

Water is essential for a garden to flourish, so an ideal sketch plan must showcase the specific areas of your house where your water sources are located. If you look closely at the sample sketch plan, you will notice that we have two downspouts, one at the upper corner of the house and the other at the bottom right. The sketch plan also indicates that the downspout at the upper corner of the house is linked to a water tap that comes right below it.

Slope

If your property is on a less steep slope, it's not much of a concern. However, if the reverse is the case for you like we have in the sample sketch plan, then you have to indicate the part of your fence on your garden that has a downward slope. But, again, remember that you are only drawing your sketch plan, so for now, you do not need to measure your slope.

Electric Meter

You probably have noticed the circular symbol behind the house that we labeled "electric meter." Why is this important to identify in a garden plan? Sometimes, you may have service people who come to read your electric meters. Thus, including the location of that particular element in your sketch plan will help ensure that you are conscious not to put anything that can block their access.

Creating an Accurate Site Survey

Having done a rough sketch of all the necessary elements of your property, you can now easily proceed to the site survey. While a sketch plan does not require any form of measurement or scale, a site survey does.

Basically, your site survey will be a scale drawing of a sketch plan. Drawing your sketch plan to scale involves putting the property elements in the right locations based on their distances. Seems like a lot to digest, right? Trust me, it's something you can do on your own. Let's look at the details involved.

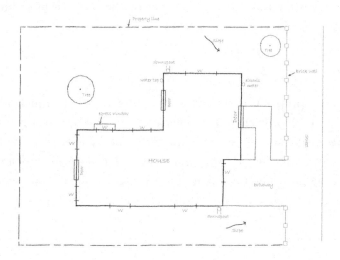

Stage 01

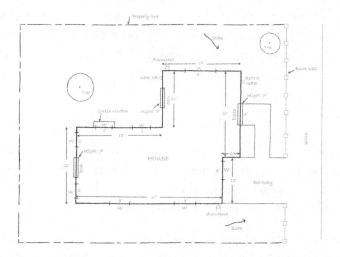

Stage 02

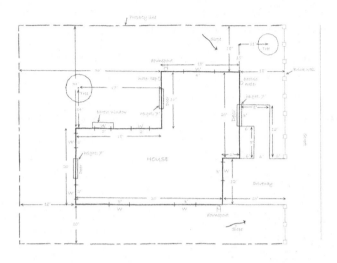

Stage 03

Measure Appropriately

An ideal way to begin your site survey process is to grab your tape and start measuring! Firstly, let's concentrate on the house. Start by measuring the overall length and width as well as the walls and boundaries of the house. After that, you can measure individual elements like the windows, doors, etc.

Once you have obtained the measurements of everything related to your house, you turn your attention to your property boundaries. For example, when measuring the length of your garden area's boundary walls or fences, you must measure each corner of the backyard from two different locations. What's the point of this? As much as we would desire a perfectly square outdoor space for our garden, it is rarely ever the case. Thus, taking corner measurements from two locations in your backyard allows you to cross-check the exact position of each corner instead of just assuming that everything runs parallel to the house.

Every measurement you take has to be included in your site survey. So if you measure the width of your window to 30cm, then write right in front or beside the area of the paper where you sketch that particular window. The same goes for every other part of the house and your outdoor space.

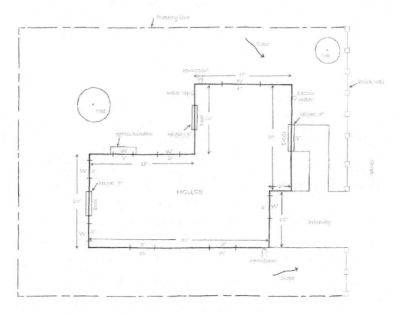

Figure 4: Adding accurate measurements to a sketch plan

Measuring Your Slope

If you discover that your garden is sloping, you will need to observe and note the beginning and the end of any slopes and the height differences. So, for instance, if your backyard has fence panels of different heights, you just have to measure the height difference of the slopes all the way down the garden. Afterward, you can put together the measurements you have taken to determine the overall height difference from one end of your backyard wall or fence to the other. Measuring your slope is essential because then you will understand your drainage system properly.

Scale

Now that you have all the measurements you need on your sketch plan, it is time to draw up a proper site survey plan that showcases all the information you have gathered. Essentially, this particular drawing must be drawn on a graph and to scale.

To draw your design plan to scale, you need graph paper. Mind you, it does not matter what type of graph paper you will be using; what is most important here is that the graph type is simple enough for you to understand what you are doing. As I stated earlier, drawing to scale is much easier than you think, so relax and let's get on with it!

Though our concern here is on how to choose the correct scale for your garden design, there is no specific type of scale that works for all property sizes. The right scale for your property is defined by its ability to ensure that your property size fits appropriately on the graph paper. In addition, the correct scale should make it easy to include all the elements and their proper proportions.

With the overall measurement of the length and width of your property, you can approximate the area that your property will occupy on graph paper. So, for example, if your property line/backyard fence is 45 feet in length and your graph paper is 30 squares wide, you might use a scale where every square on the graph paper equals 2 feet on the ground. This means that your graph paper would represent the fence as 22.5 squares.

Not to worry; this is the only point you will be doing math in the process! I'm terrible at math, yet I can do this kind of scaling; so if a novice like me can do it, you can too!

Plotting

Using whatever scale you've chosen, you can begin plotting what you have on your sketch plan on your graph paper. Mind you, this time, you have to consider each element's measurement.

It is highly recommended that you begin the plotting process by using dots first to identify the corners where each property area should be located on the graph. Then you can use a ruler to connect the dots you have plotted. This will make your survey plan look slightly neater than your sketch plan.

In the last seven years of helping people design their gardens, I have worked with many people who end up with garden designs they don't want. Interestingly, every time I try to find out what went wrong, the answers always boil down to the fact that the majority of garden designers in these situations do not plan. They do not put in much thought at the very beginning, and their neglect becomes an obstacle later in their design process.

Fortunately for you, this chapter provides you with all the necessary information you need to know to understand what a sketch plan is and what it involves, as well as what a site survey is and how to draw a scale plan. Indeed, understanding and implementing the lessons from this chapter right from the start will make you a near-genius in the world of garden design. So take your time and learn at your own pace. If you are unable to get it right with your first attempt, please do not be discouraged because, trust me, in no time, you will become a pro at creating your own masterpiece of a garden.

Chapter Summary

- The core stages of garden design do not require fancy design tools but just the drawing skills of an eight-year-old.
- The first step of garden design is creating a site survey which you might find already designed in the mortgage documents of your property. If not, you will have to design it from scratch using a sketch plan.
- The site survey is a measured-to-scale drawing of the elements in your outdoor space plus the outside aspects of your house, like windows and doors.
- On the other hand, a sketch plan is simply a rough drawing of your outdoor space without any specifications or measurements.
- When creating a sketch plan, it is best to start with the boundaries of the properties, the slopes, the house itself, its windows and doors, as well as the water taps and electric meters.
- To replicate your sketch plan, you must measure every identified element as appropriately as possible. Then you can choose the scale that will ensure your property size fits properly on the graph paper.

NOTES

6

Your Garden's Problems

Gardeners, I think, dream bigger than emperors.

Mary Cantwell

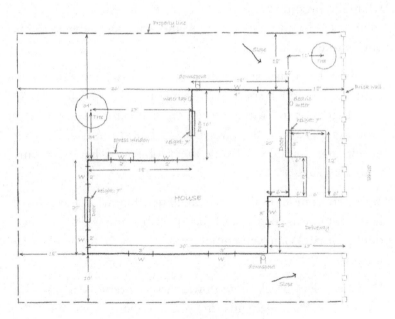

(Image: Site Survey)

Having drawn your site survey following the simple steps we discussed in the last chapter, you can confidently proceed to the next stages of the garden design process. Always remember that with every step, you are getting closer to realizing the ultimate goal of creating your perfect garden design. So, please stick with me!

We established in the previous chapter that the site survey involves sketching on paper the different elements of your property in the right locations using a particular scale. But before we get into the next steps, let me emphasize that you must create several copies of your now completed site survey. For this chapter alone, you will need two separate copies for site inventory and site analysis.

Pronouncing the words is quite a mouthful, isn't it? Simply put, your site inventory is everything in your outdoor space. So keep the word "inventory" in mind when trying to figure out what site inventory means. At a store, "inventory" means all their stock. In this case, a site inventory is everything (stock) in your garden (store).

On the other hand, site analysis involves fixing your problems with your outdoor space. For example, if a specific part of your garden is too windy (problem), you can raise your fence (solution). That's it. So, always keep that at the back of your mind: Site analysis = fixing the problems I have with my outdoor space.

Yes, there is more to these two activities than what I explained here. But if you keep what I just described in your mind, then don't worry. Whatever comes next will be a piece of cake for you.

Well then, let's break them down! A site inventory is simply a list of essential elements in your property that must be addressed when creating your garden design. These elements include everything that currently exists on your property. In some cases, certain elements from your neighbors' property may also be included if they have the possibility of influencing your design.

How is a site inventory different from a site survey? Think of it as a well-detailed road map of your property, with additional information on its climatic and environmental factors. So when creating your site inventory, you are expected not just to list out the hardscaping features on your property; you also have to mark out information about the sun angle, wind direction, and drainage patterns. Since I'm also a visual learner I've of course included a sketch of how to create your site inventory On page ... for you to look at.

So is that all we will be doing in this chapter? Not at all! Having identified all the elements on your property and having sketch them into your site inventory, our next step will be to do a site analysis of that inventory. Site analysis involves evaluating and judging all the features and elements you have identified in your site inventory. During the evaluation, you also figure out the unique problem areas associated with your property and develop ideas to resolve these problems. So, for instance, you might discover from your site inventory that you have no high fences in your backyard, and you certainly do not want any nosy neighbors looking at you when you sunbathe. You take care of issues like this during your site analysis.

I know this might seem like a lot to take in, and it's completely okay if you're feeling that way right now. Based on the less complex explanation I gave initially, review the sketches, and you will be flying. Essentially, conducting a thoughtful inventory and analysis gives you the chance to ensure that your garden design contains only features that would be useful and desirable. It offers you a solid foundation on which you can create a more functional and wonderful garden. Remember that saying, "A stitch in time saves nine?" Doing a site inventory and a site analysis builds you into an oracle who foresees and resolves all the likely loopholes that could become problematic during the actual design. How magical is that? Well, without further ado, let's get started!

Creating Your Site inventory

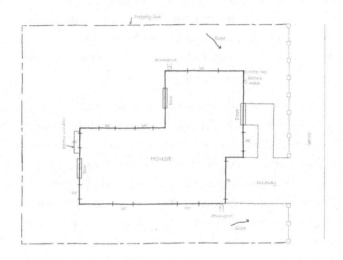

Site Inventory_Step 01

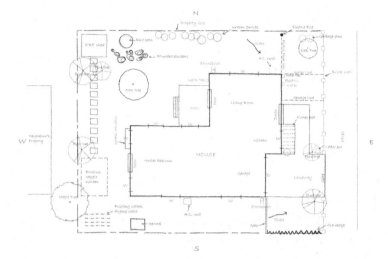

Site Inventory_Step 02

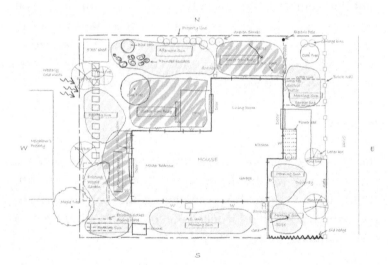

Site Inventory_Step 03

Like we said earlier, creating a site survey involves you walking around your property both within and outside and then sketching out every element that currently exists on the property. To make your site inventory, you will use a copy of the site survey you created in the last chapter. As you probably have noticed, step 1 in site inventory does not include the measurements from our site survey copy. I have done this to make things look more clear in a sketch form for you to look at. Meaning that you don't have to exclude the measurements from your site survey unless you also need to do so for clarity's sake. As stated above, make serval copies of site survey so they are ready to use for steps 2 and 3, which we will now discuss.

To make this chapter just as practical as the previous one, I have created a sample diagram of what your site inventory should look like at the end of the day, which you see above. Nevertheless, please understand that this particular sample seems quite neat. When drawing your site inventory, the messier you are, the better your work. So if you realize at any point that your sketch seems to be getting rough or messy, you are doing a good job! Besides, the goal of this chapter is not to groom you into a professional garden designer but instead to make you a gardener who can create an accurate site inventory. So what does a site inventory involve?

Orientation

Once you have your site survey spread out in front of you, it is best to establish which sides of your property are to the north, south, east, and west. For example, on the sample diagram above, you will see that I labelled the four sides with the letters N, W, E, and S.

Hardscape Features and Existing Plants

You will recall that in chapter 3, we discussed that hardscaping features refer to all the physical elements you can see as you walk around your entire property, whether they are made of stone, brick, concrete, wood, metal, etc. You will also realize that when creating our site survey, we focused more on the boundary features like your property lines, fences, doors, windows, brick walls, etc. However, in the case of this site inventory, you will need to identify most, if not all, of the hardscape features on and around your property.

While identifying the hardscape features on your property, you must also make an inventory of the existing plants on it. If you are wondering what use such information will be, keep in mind that while some of these existing trees could help provide shade and protection for your garden, others may not be beneficial to your garden design plan, as they could be hazardous or in poor health. So, listing all the existing plants in your site inventory will make your job easier during site analysis, where you will make certain important decisions.

Let's analyze the landscaping features and existing plants on the sample site inventory. To the east, we have a gate that leads straight into the driveway, with a pine tree on either side. Moving upward towards the north, we have a flower bed right behind one of the windows. Some feet away from the flower bed, there is an oak tree at the very last end with two garbage bins in front. As you move from the oak tree towards the north, you find an electric pole with some uneven shrubs and rounded boulders a few feet away from the pole. Finally, a five-by-five-foot shed is at the far corner right before the birdbath.

Imagine standing right in front of the shed and looking towards the south. You will see two pine trees (big and small) behind each other along the pathway leading to a small veggie garden. In front of this existing veggie garden is another pine tree, and on the side of the garden is a maple tree that leads outside the property and separates it from its neighbor's. On the southern side of the property, you see an existing clothesline and a pet kennel. Moving towards the east, you will notice a gate leading to an area fenced with old hedges.

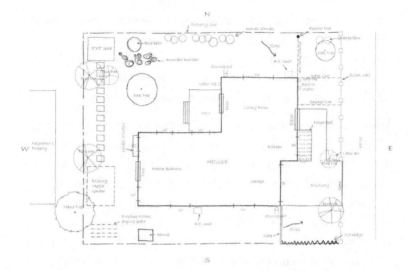

At this point, you will notice that we have not said anything about the house in the center of the sample inventory. Well, we have not forgotten about it. Unlike what we have in the site survey, several elements have now been included in the house structure. Looking at the diagram, you will realize that we have located the house's different rooms and two AC units. The home also has a smaller patio right in front. With that, we have covered all this property's built features!

Sun and Shade

Having identified your property's hardscaping features and its existing plants, the next important element your site inventory must include is the path of sunlight in your outdoor space. Let's take a quick walk down memory lane. You will recall that we discussed extensively how important it is for your overall garden design plan to be influenced by how the sun affects your outdoor space throughout the different seasons.

Well, I have good news for you! You will not have to go through the basic process of observation again. Remember the little fun practice in chapter 2 where you had to make several sketches of your outdoor space in the morning, afternoon, and evening? In those sketches, you highlighted the specific areas that are the sunniest, as well as the shaded areas with the least amount of direct sunlight. Well, it is time to grab those sketches or notes, as you will be incorporating the information you have on them into your site inventory.

It's pretty straightforward; all you have to do is follow the sample diagram above. Using a yellow highlighter, highlight the sunny spots in your garden. Then use a pen or pencil to shade the areas with the least sunlight.

In our sample site inventory, five specific areas, including the driveways and veggie garden area, were highlighted with the label "Morning sun." In the north, we have more afternoon sun; towards the west, we have the evening sun shining all over the pathway between the shed and the veggie garden. Similarly, the site inventory also located the three shaded areas of the property that receive the least direct sunlight.

Wind

Incorporating information about your area's wind flow patterns in your site inventory is good. However, this information is not as important as locating the sunniest and shadiest spots in your outdoor space; after all, they are the center of your outdoor space (you know, helping your plants grow and all). You will definitely breeze with ease (pun intended) through this step because another task you did in chapter 2 was observe how wind direction naturally shifts in your space with the seasons. You will remember that I recommended you ask your older neighbors if the neighborhood is typically stormy; they would know, having lived in the community longer.

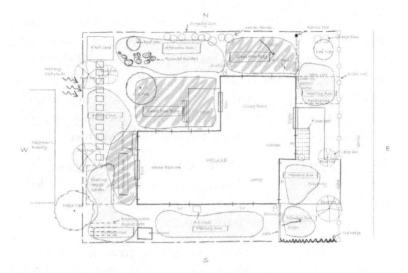

If you did the little fun exercise and wrote down the direction and speed of wind flow patterns in your area, you can now include this information on your site inventory. Voila! Looking at our sample below, you will see a set of zig-zag arrows with the label "Westerly cold winds." It simply means that cold winds tend to blow in from the west for such an area.

Utilities

Another important thing you do not want to miss when creating your site inventory is the utilities. These utilities are usually erected with lines that are buried very shallowly. None of us want to be victims of something as dangerous as digging near underground gas or electric lines. As such, you must identify the different important utilities on your property, whether electric meters, wells, septic tanks, phone cables, water taps, etc. Afterward, you are to mark the locations of these identified utility lines on the site inventory sketch. With such information, you are better guided when deciding your plant and hardscape locations.

Let's refer back to our sample diagram. Above the flower bed we have on the east, you will see the sewage line and the water line that leads from the water taps. The inventory also locates the electric power line that connects the electric pole to the house.

If you find it hard to locate these important utility lines on your own, you can easily contact your local utility companies to help identify them. You may also find such information on your mortgage documents, so check there first. And in some states (like Georgia, for example), you can take advantage of free utility location services. You cannot afford to compromise on accuracy or guess the locations of these utility lines, so make sure you get this step exactly right.

Drainage

In chapter 2, we described the different types of soil and their unique features, one of which was the moisture level of each soil (that is, how much water it holds). We also emphasized that depending on the moisture level, soil water availability in your area is critical to your plant selection process.

The downspout locations and drain patterns in your property determine the soil water availability on your property; hence, these elements must be properly located on your site inventory. Since you already understand how you can test and identify the soil type in your garden area, identifying these important elements in your site inventory will guide you better when you have to determine the plants to be selected for gardening, and the best way to group them according to their water spots.

Creating Site Analysis

After you have successfully made a detailed inventory of all the elements you have on your property, you can move to the next stage, site analysis (which is finding solutions to the problems in your outdoor space). As we stated in the introduction of this chapter, this stage is more of an evaluation process where you get to judge all the information you have recorded from your site inventory. In the evaluation process, you will identify the different problem areas on your site and the areas with design opportunities where you can locate new features.

Don't forget that every site comes with its typical issues. Thus, the primary goal of your site analysis is to determine and develop creative actions that can be taken to both resolve your problem areas as well as appropriately take advantage of positive aspects. Generally, a successful site analysis will seek to provide answers to these five questions:

- What are my opportunities and constraints?
- What do I wish to keep?
- What will be removed?
- What needs to be changed or modified?
- What will be added? That is, what do you need to include to fix a problem?

But before we discuss the steps involved in site analysis, I must remind you that, just like your site inventory, it is absolutely alright if your site analysis looks really messy. Your major focus here should be on how best you can resolve problems. One piece of advice I tend to give gardeners whom I have helped to create garden designs is that site analysis is not set in stone. As such, you just have to tap into your unique creativity and find solutions to the different problems on your property. Therefore you will probably make multiple sketches which is great, when using your creative side you will have multiple great ideas and also not so great ideas on how to solve certain problems.

Sketch all of those ideas and when you have exhausted each option you can make a fresh site analysis where you leave out the "bad" ideas and only put in the best. This is so your sketch looks more uncluttered and is easier to look at.

Typical site analysis.

Now how does this whole thing work? First, you need to pull out another copy of your site survey and place it beside your site inventory. Now, you will recall that in the first chapter of this book, you had to create a table where you listed out your garden design wants and needs. Well, we are going to need that list here, as it will go a long way in helping you make the best decisions during your site analysis. You may even end up getting your best solutions from the list.

Did I hear somebody say, "Oh no! I haven't done it yet! Well, that is fine! Take time to create and update your list of wants and needs. Make sure to revisit Chapter 1, so you can tell your needs apart from your wants. Knowing which of your desires is either a want or a need is important.

So how do you then utilize the information from your site inventory and wants and needs lists to do your site analysis? First, let's break down the sample diagram we have above to see how I was able to identify both the positive aspects and problem areas from the site inventory we created, and how I came up with creative ideas to resolve these problems while still incorporating my wants and needs into the analysis.

Hedges

Looking at the sample, the first problem I see is towards the west, so follow me! Looking at the cold winds that come from the west, it is certain that my garden and patio areas will be quite vulnerable to the effects of the cold. As such, I devised an effective solution to plant hedges right in front of the house to block the cold winds from getting to my patio and veggie garden.

Shed Transformation

On the northwest lane, our site inventory identified a five-by-five-foot shed in the corner of the property. So I wondered, "Does it stay or do we remove it?" Actually, it could be of great use, so let's leave it as an experimental space for now. I could use it as a storage space for our gardening tools and equipment.

Existing Garden Space

The size of my existing garden space is another heavy problem for me. Resolving this issue is quite simple, as all I have to do is to extend it by a few feet. Mind you, I am not really making any exact measurements at this point. Instead, I focus more on incorporating my ideas into my site analysis.

But my problem is not fully solved even after extending the size of my garden area because the garden is still open to the prying eyes of my neighbors. So what do I do to ensure my privacy? Oh yes! Erecting a living wall to fence the garden could work perfectly, and you see it on the sketch!

Pathways

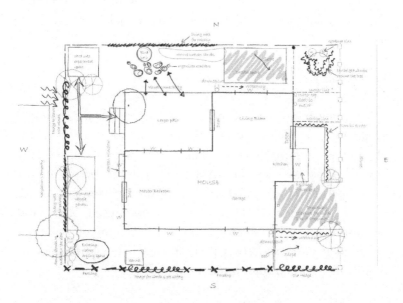

In our site inventory, we also identified a pathway that leads from the shed to the veggie garden. So to take things a level higher, I decided to scrap out that two-way path and replace it with a three-way path that connects the shed and the veggie garden as well as to the door of the larger patio. This way, I can move easily from the patio to either of these places. Sounds cool, right?

Patio

Let's link all we've learned so far and see how they play a role in your site analysis. For instance, one of my garden design goals is to create a larger patio where my family and I can sit and enjoy the fresh air. To achieve this goal, I have to enlarge the small patio I identified in my site inventory. However, as much as I want my patio to be an ideal relaxation spot, I also need it to have some privacy. Fortunately, I already have an oak tree just a few feet away. So, all I have to do is to ensure that the small patio is enlarged to have the oak tree serving as its shade.

Boulders and Uneven Shrubs

On the left-hand side of my patio, we have some rounded boulders and uneven shrubs that do not look so attractive along the property line. To make this area more visually appealing, so the view from my patio will also be pleasing, I thought it would be great to remove the uneven shrubs but keep the boulders to be organized and reused later. And because I am still so keen on improving the privacy of both my garden and property, I realized that it would be nice to build a living wall right on the property line.

Shaded Area

Since the living wall erected on the property line will not cover the area of the house facing the living room, I thought I might as well create a shaded space on the free land area in front of the living room window.

Shrub Borders

Moving on, I discovered that some of the trees identified in the site inventory require special attention. For instance, I may want to add small shrubs to maintain the view of the maple tree that extends from my property to that of my neighbor. Also, the oak tree close to the electric pole could look more beautiful with some low-height shrubs, so I did the honors and incorporated it there.

Fencing

By now, you should be seeing that privacy is a key need in this sample site analysis. However, you can see that on the site inventory, the southern side of the property is quite open to everyone's view. The fact that we have an existing clothesline and a kennel for pets in that area is not too good. Thus, for shade, privacy and pet safety, I will build a fence for the area where we have the drying space and then use an old hedge to protect the kennel. The rest of the house on the south side will be fenced.

Waterways

Right from our site survey, we identified two downspouts on this site, one on the roof of the house and the other on the ground. These two vertical pipes must have waterways that enable the water that is being drained to move freely. Hence, I took note of that in my site analysis.

Driveway

Finally, I could not resist the temptation of upgrading my driveway to a carport. By doing so, I am sure that my cars and that of my family members will be better maintained under a roof that protects them from bird droppings and provides adequate shade.

And there you have the full breakdown of the sample site analysis diagram! At this point, you hopefully agree that conducting site inventory and analysis is not as difficult as it might seem initially. Getting the job done takes a little effort, focus, and creativity.

Essentially, I have discovered from experience that most of us tend to think of creativity as a rare quality exclusive to a particular set of people. Fortunately, this assumption is completely wrong. We all have the unique ability to come up with practical and creative solutions. Therefore, I want you to look beyond your fears and begin to see how you will go about your site inventory and site analysis as your chance to create all the magic that you want your garden and even your entire property to have.

It is perfectly fine if you have to make multiple sketches before you get it right. The first time I drafted my site analysis, I ended up with eight different sketches, and seven of those went in the trash can. I could only get a final sketch that looked like something I could work with after taking a step back and not overthinking the process. SO my tip here is, don't overthink! Not even about ensuring the lines are straight. Just get your idea on paper. Whatever you pen down isn't concrete or final. You can always go back and adjust.

Chapter Summary

- Having created your site survey, first, make several copies of it, then proceed to create your site inventory and site analysis.
- A site inventory involves identifying all the important elements in your property on a copy of your already designed site survey, while site analysis is the evaluation and judgment of all the features and elements you have identified in your site inventory.
- When creating your site inventory, you must identify the appropriate orientations of your property, utilities, hardscaping features and existing plants located in it, as well as the sun and wind paths.
- Once you have completed your site inventory, then you can identify the problem areas and opportunity areas in them.
- With your needs and wants list right by your side, create your site analysis while incorporating different creative ideas to resolve the problem areas and take proper advantage of your opportunity areas.

NOTES

7

Final Design Steps

"Life begins the day you start a garden."

Chinese proverb

Whew! From the foundational level that mainly requires research to creating your site survey, site inventory, and site analysis, you and I have come a long way! Honestly, I understand that the journey to this point might have been a little overwhelming for you; but believe me, you are closer to achieving your ultimate goal than ever imagined! So hang in there, and let's get through the last few steps you need to understand to become a pro at designing!

In the last chapter, we covered quite a lot, from identifying all the elements on your property and incorporating the sun/wind patterns in your site inventory to figuring out the best solution to your problem areas in site analysis. By now, you will have realized that everything we discuss in earlier chapters always comes into play as we move ahead. This chapter about the final design steps is not any different. The information we gathered while creating our site inventory and site analysis will be fully utilized in the chapter.

Essentially, the final phase of the garden design process is divided into three major parts. The three basic steps in the final design process include creating a bubble plan, an exploratory design, and the final design plan. Now, I bet you are already lifting your eyebrows, confused at the strange terms I just mentioned. How about we take it one step at a time?

The Bubble Plan

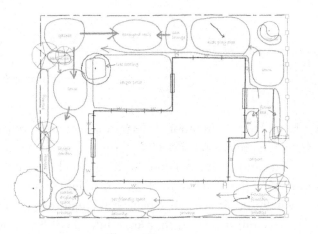

Bubble Diagram_Phase 1

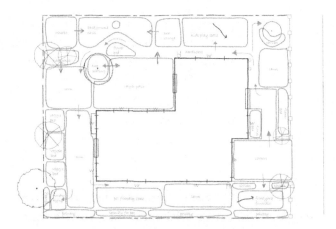

Bubble Diagram_Phase 2

The first stage of the final design process is centered on concept design, or what most call the bubble plan. As the name implies, this plan requires that you represent your most crucial garden design features using rough, loosely circular shapes—the "bubbles." Starting your final design process with a bubble plan makes it easy for you to reorganize your space to incorporate both your garden goals and the solutions to the problems in your garden you identified during your site analysis. Also, by creating a series of bubble diagrams, you will see different possibilities and even the true potential of your garden site. The thing I love most about bubble plans, and I am sure you will also come to enjoy, is that it does not include using many details or putting any effort into the drawing.

Now enough of the suspense. Let's look at the steps involved in creating your concept design. Grab your garden wants and needs list, site analysis, a blank copy of your site survey, and your sun and shade study!

Remember, I emphasized earlier that you should make several copies of your site survey. To create your bubble plan, we will need another copy of that same site survey. Also, your site analysis and list of garden design wants/needs must be placed beside you as you attempt to create your bubble plan. Having these items helps ensure you incorporate all the necessary elements into your plan. Our site analysis may or may not have contained all our garden goals. Thus, the bubble plan is a way you can explore the many design layouts your garden could have. We have a sample to guide you as we walk through these steps. So let's get into it!

Make "bubbles" for each element and label them with the functions they will serve in your design.

The tip for this step is for you to always start with the most important elements and work towards the less important ones. When drawing the bubbles, you don't have to put a lot of effort into ensuring they are perfectly shaped. What is most important is that they are rounded and filled in with words that explain what the functions of the specific spaces are meant to be.

So drawing from the important elements we identified when creating our sample site analysis, my bubble plan will include a larger patio and veggie garden, a shaded area and fence for privacy, a carpool, a kennel, etc. Apart from these architectural features, I also include important existing plants that have been identified during my site inventory and site analysis.

Just as you are trying to recreate the elements you incorporate in both your site inventory and site analysis into your bubble plan, you must also address the most important elements that need to be taken of from your list of wants and needs, and figure out where you are going to put them on the bubble plan. So, for example, I have not included anything about creating a safe play area for my kids in the design plan so far. But you will notice on the sample bubble plan that I have found a suitable, free and shaded area on the northern side, and so I drew a bubble there that represents a play area for my kids. I also added a front yard fountain at the right corner on the south. You will also see that I have decided to transform the five-by-five shed I identified in my site inventory into a gazebo. I also decided to change the other free spaces on the plan into lawns.

From my experience, I have noticed that most gardeners tend to encounter problems when creating their bubble plan because they try to visualize the finished garden, which is not the point of creating a bubble plan. At this stage, you are only working with the big concepts. Therefore your goal should be to try as many design layouts as you see fit (at least three). Finally, it would be best if you exhausted all the options in which your garden could look great so that you won't have missed out on a great design.

Mind you; you have the chance to switch the location of the features as many times as you want. So see, for instance, how I changed the location of my drying space because I figured it looks better when the arrangement aligns well with my vegetable garden.

Think about how your bubbles will be connected.

When you are satisfied with the number of bubbles you have used to fill up different areas on your plan, the next important question is how you get from one bubble point to another. As much as we would love to draw bubbles to indicate the pathways, doing so could make things a little complex. Just like this:

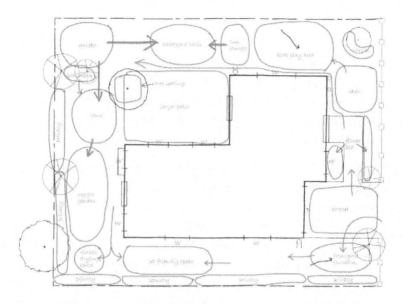

Image: of Bubble Plan

You should represent your connecting pathways with solid or dashed arrows. Take a look at the sample site analysis we worked on in the previous chapter, for example. You will see that we came up with the solution of creating a three-way path that connects the shed and the veggie garden to each other and to the large patio we have in front of the house. So having identified those elements using bubbles, we simply use a solid or dashed arrow to connect the three bubbles. At this point, I want to remind you that providing enough suitable pathways that enable people to move with ease within your garden and property is just as important as figuring out the attractive features that should be included in your outdoor space.

Make multiple designs

As I have repeatedly said throughout this guide, it is absolutely fine if your design does not make sense to you initially. The best thing you can do is create multiple bubble plans (they are effortless, so in reality, it isn't a lot of work). When you let your creativity have fun in your design, you'll soon come across a design that feels right. But keep in mind the importance of the sun and shade study when coming up with different designs. While garden design is the goal, we don't want a situation where you end up with a design without putting some elements in the right place. For instance, a veggie bed could look really nice in a particular place in your garden, like your patio, but then there isn't enough sunlight reaching the veggie bed. What do you get? A non-growing veggie bed. So, take note of your sun and shade study in your designs.

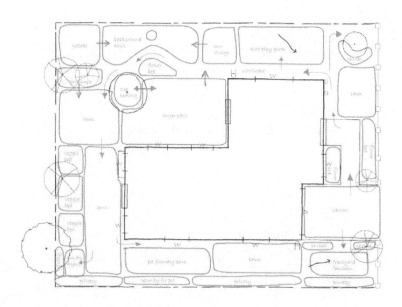

Please do not be intimidated by the thought of having to make more designs. Instead, you should look at the bright side and tell yourself, "It is better to fail on paper than in real life, as the latter is quite difficult and costly to rectify." So take your time to get this step right by creating as many bubble plans as you want. Then pick out the one you like best in your garden because your choice will be the basis for the next step we will discuss.

Exploratory Design Plan

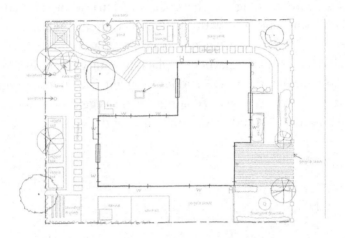

Exploratory Diagram_Phase 1

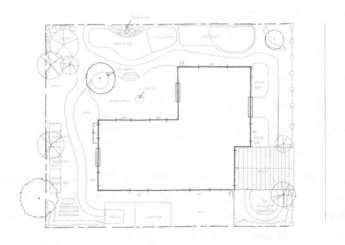

Exploratory Diagram_Phase 2

When creating our bubble plans, we were more focused on working with the big concepts, and the only result the bubble plan has to offer is a rough idea of where things will be positioned in your outdoor space and how much space they are likely to use. However, at this point where you have completed your bubble plan, you may begin to ask yourself questions like, "What exactly is going to be included in each bubble space? What materials would they be made of? And most importantly, what exact shapes and forms will the design elements take?" Not all of our garden features will be in bubble shapes in their final forms! Believe it or not, this is what I thought for a minute when I was first introduced to this design style. (Alright, laugh at me if you want.)

An exploratory design is more detailed but preliminary to the final design plan of your garden. It's called "exploratory" because you explore different angles and shapes. So unlike the bubble plan, you can look at a finished exploratory design plan and visualize an image of the finished design. Additionally, at the point of creating the exploratory design, you begin to make more refined decisions concerning the suitable shape of your design elements, the materials to be used, and even their functions.

A quick reminder before we examine the steps for creating an exploratory design. If you can come up with great ideas that you want to add or change in your bubble plan, you are free to do so. However, you must always keep your garden design wants and needs in the back of your mind, as a well-designed exploratory plan includes most, if not all, of the garden's design, wants, and needs. Now that we have gotten that out of the way let's pick up another blank copy of our site survey and examine the best approach for making a preliminary design plan for your garden.

Pick your chosen garden design style and mood board.

To create an even more effective exploratory design plan, you must consider the type of garden style you have chosen for your garden. In chapter 3, we explored different garden styles, including formal and informal, climate-oriented, and wildlife styles. We also discussed how you could create a garden mood board where you have pictures, materials that efficiently convey your chosen garden style, and what you want to see in your final design.

You may need to have these elements (garden style and mood board) worked out and ready for use before you begin your exploratory design plan. They will go a long way in providing you with the needed inspiration and insights at this stage of the design process that you need to create a unique and perfect garden. Imagine designing your exploratory plan without having an idea of the garden style you want your garden to depict or how you envision your garden to look.

Work with different shapes.

There are several approaches to creating an effective exploratory design plan. However, we will stick to a simple yet very practical approach, which is the shape-based approach.

This approach involves using just one shape at a time to design your entire exploratory plan. The idea here is that by using one shape at a time, you will be able to create cohesiveness in your garden plan so that every part of the plan is functionally related to each other or look like each other. You can make as many exploratory plans as you want using different shapes. In the sample, you will see two different shapes (circles and rectangles) to create two other exploratory plans.

So let's start with a circle! You will remember that a larger patio space is one of the important elements we identified in our bubble plan. So imagine, for instance, that I want my garden to have a woodland design style, and on my garden mood board, I have a wonderful photo of a curved and raised patio area that is made out of wood. Using that photo as a guide, I will draw a circular patio with stone-like pathways, with a fire pit right in the middle.

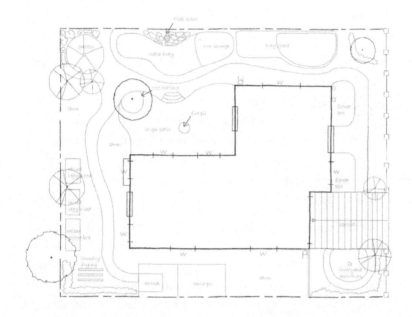

Following the same steps, you can easily recreate everything you have on your bubble plan into your exploratory garden plan. However, this time you have your garden mood board to help you be more specific about what you want in each of those spaces and the materials you want them to be made of. But if you didn't end up drawing up a mood board (because, let's face it, it can be tiring), then that's fine also. Your garden goals will give you an idea of how to make do without the mood board. Do you want a fountain? Where? Here the SMR formula gives you all the details to these kind of questions which makes putting them into your design so simple.

Also, it would help if you remembered this time as you draw each element that you need to get the size approximately correct. How do you do so? It is quite simple. Remember that you have been working with your site survey that already has a scale. So in my case, each box on my site survey graph equals 2 feet. So all I have to do is to estimate the measurement of the space that will be suitable for my purpose and try to implement this in my exploratory plan.

Now away from what we have on the bubble plan, you might also have certain garden wants that you have still not included in the plan. At this point you can try to incorporate them into the suitable free spaces you have in your exploratory design plan. As you begin to identify all the elements and how they are connected using pathways on your exploratory design plan, you will start to visualize the image of a finalized garden. Isn't that exciting?

However, you should not forget that we are taking it one shape at a time, so do not be too quick to make your pick! So pick up another copy of your site survey, and let's make another exploratory plan using the same bubble plan as your basic outline. However, this time you will use rectangles and straight lines instead of the circular patio and curved pathways I made in my previous exploratory plan.

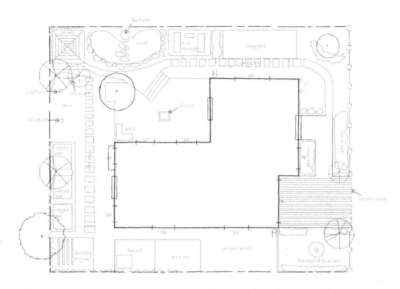

Like in the bubble plan, it is great if you do multiple designs of your exploratory plan. Always keep in mind that it is the plan of your garden that contains features you may change in your final design plan. As such, trial and error are okay at this point.

Know that you can use whichever shape you can think of. The sketches provided in this book are just examples, an inspiration to get your creative juices flowing. In fact, forging ahead with any shape will help punctuate the uniqueness of your garden.

ISABELLA WOODS

The Final Design Plan

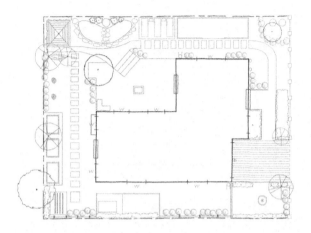

Detail Design_Phase 01

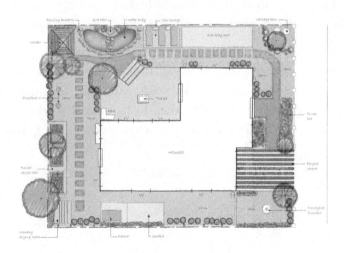

Detail Design_Phase 02

Did I also mention that you just received the determination award? (Yes, I made that up.) We've just reached the final part of the actual design process!

Creating the final design requires that you provide more detail to your exploratory plan, fine-tune every part of your design, and ensure the size of all the design elements is accurate, no matter how insignificant you think it is. Let's break it down as we examine the simple steps to create your final design plan.

Get a bigger piece of paper.

Up to this point, we have done all our drawing on the same-sized pieces of paper. However, for the final design plan, it is highly recommended that you switch to a bigger piece of paper. Now, doing so will mean a change in scale. So in my case, I have been using a scale of 1 square to 2 feet. However, I may decide to switch to a scale of 1 square to 1 foot. This means that I will have to get four pieces of graph paper and tape them together. What is the point of using a bigger piece of paper for your final design? Well, it simply enables you to achieve more accuracy and detail.

Pick your best exploratory plan.

Now back to the exploratory design! Exploratory plans with rectangles are usually the ones that are well-laid out with a formal garden style. You can tell from the sample that it is quite a neat layout that requires low maintenance. So I personally would pick the exploratory design made with rectangles over the one I made with circles.

Transform it into your final design!

To transform our preferred exploratory design into a final design plan, we need to fine-tune our decisions and make the drawing of each element a little bit more accurate. Even elements as simple as the pathways I have on the west must be measured correctly on the site survey graph. I have to decide how wide that pathway will be and then measure the exact number of feet on paper. Now, if you look closely at the sample of my final design, you will see that I specified what each area would be made of. For example, it is obvious from the design of my carport that it will be made of wood, with most of the outdoor space covered with grass except the area where I have designed pathways to allow for easy movement through the space.

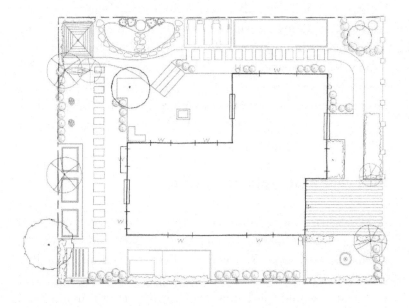

Now let's focus on the northern side of the design plan because it is a fascinating part for me. The first thing you will likely see is the gazebo that will be made with vertical wood to keep it airy and spacious. And right beside is the sensational view of my backyard oasis, well-surrounded and decorated with the boulders I identified as reusable in my site analysis. I put them to good use, didn't I? Moving forward, I have my sun lounge quite close to my kids play area, so I can properly monitor them when enjoying a bit of Vitamin D with my family and friends.

Apart from this part of the garden, my large patio with a firepit placed right in the center is another attractive area. If you didn't notice my gardening space, I have decided to opt for raised veggie beds, as they are a better option for proper drainage.

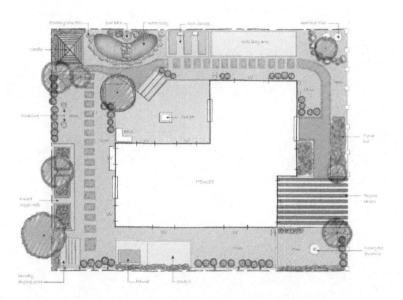

And there you have the details of my final design plan! I know this looks neat and pretty, but you shouldn't feel intimidated if you can't draw that well.

Hopefully, you will agree that the sample design we have just created is a functional garden that requires relatively low maintenance but still has enough space for planting. Now you can see that all the steps we highlighted, from creating a bubble plan to making your final garden design, are pretty easy to understand. I am quite aware that the information may be too much to handle at once, so please just take it one step at a time. Trust me, and if you do so, you will easily get to understand the whole process better than you ever imagined.

Following and implementing the simple steps discussed in the three sections of this chapter is your direct ticket to achieving your ultimate dream of creating a perfect garden design that is pleasing and attractive to the eyes but also functional. So take those final steps with courage and bring your vision to reality.

Chapter Summary

- The final design phase involves three basic steps: creating a bubble plan, making an exploratory design plan, and finally wrapping up the final design plan.
- A bubble plan is created using rough, loosely circular bubbles to represent your most important garden design features.
- You do not visualize the detailed results at this stage but concentrate on working with big concepts.
- On the other hand, creating an exploratory design plan requires that you recreate your bubble plan while including details concerning the suitable shape of your design elements, the materials to be used, and even their functions in more detail.
- Explanatory plans are made using a shape-based approach involving drawing your property's different elements in circular and rectangular forms.
- It is better to fail on paper than in real life, as the latter is quite difficult and costly, so making multiple designs of either your bubble plan or exploratory plan is completely okay.
- To create your final design plan, you have to select your best exploratory plan, give it some details, and then make sure that the size of all the design elements is accurate.

NOTES

PART III

Post-Design

PUT AWAY YOUR SCISSORS AND GET OUT YOUR GLOVES

8

The Best Plants for You

"Gardening simply does not allow one to be mentally old because too many hopes and dreams are yet to be realized."

Allan Armitage

People tend to have beautiful dreams of what they want to achieve. However, many lack the courage to go ahead and fight for those dreams. However, in your case, not only did you have a dream of creating your ideal garden design, you went right ahead and designed it! That's the definition of living the dream.

As much as I want to say that my job here is done and bid you farewell as you begin your journey of achieving more gardening goals, there are quite a few loose ends we need to sew up to ensure that you get a garden that is not only well-designed but also functional on all levels, especially in terms of having the best plants.

The first thing most people begin to think of after completing their garden design is how they can fill up that beautiful work of art with the best and most aesthetically pleasing plants. Trust me. I know how exciting that feeling can be! But, nonetheless, I need you to pause and do some research! Now, I know you might think, "Oh, come on, Isabella! What is possibly left to research? We've come such a long way already!" Well, maybe now is the perfect time to share another one of my gardening mistakes with you.

After I completed the design of my very first garden, just like you might be feeling at this point, I was so excited to get my garden space up and running with the best kinds of plants. I did not waste time and just went shopping for different plant seeds and seedlings. I was utterly clueless about what to consider before making my decisions; as such, I could not help but be tempted to buy the beautiful and colorful transplants I saw in the nurseries.

I brought my selected seeds and seedlings home, only to realize after a few weeks that they were indeed the wrong choice for my garden. You can imagine how such an incident would have dampened the mood of an excited beginner. Nonetheless, I realized that my plant selection process also demands a little research, just like I did before creating my garden design. Therefore, the goal of this chapter is to guide you to make sure that you do not make the same mistake I did.

The post-design stage involves selecting plants to fill your perfectly designed garden. To a large extent, plants—including vegetables, flowers, and herbs—are responsible for giving life to the beautiful masterpiece you have already created. See how high of relevance they have to your garden? Hence, choosing the most suitable plants for your garden is important, as it will enable you to maximize their use while still witnessing their healthy growth through the season.

How to Fill Your Garden Properly

At this point, the first thing I need you to understand is that you cannot grow just any type of plant in your garden and expect it to germinate healthy enough to improve the aesthetics of your garden. Instead, it would help if you found the **right** plants for your garden to get those results.

But before we go into that, I would like to emphasize that every season is a learning experience for gardeners because they each come with their challenges and successes. By knowing and practicing the steps we are about to discuss, you can start your planting season on the right foot. That way, you can minimize the future struggles you are likely to face. Now that we have gotten that out, let's consider the following factors.

Climate

Remember, in Chapter 2. We identified climate as one of the environmental factors that must be considered before you begin your garden design plan. You will also have to reconsider that particular factor after completing your garden design. However, this time you will aim to ascertain which plants are most likely to grow best in your garden.

Our first points of consideration regarding climate are sunlight and shade. Of course, every vegetable, fruit, and herb requires sunlight to thrive. However, the specific amount needed by each plant tends to differ. For example, while some plants may require at least four hours of direct sunshine a day, others might demand eight or more.

Fortunately for you, we have already spent a great deal of effort figuring out how much direct sun and shade gets to the different parts of your garden in a day. With that information at hand, you can simply list out the types of plants you would prefer to grow in your garden, and then try to see if their sunlight and shade requirements are feasible with what is available. For example, we have some cool-season crops like spinach, cabbage and radishes that can grow quite well in partial shade, defined as an area that gets between 3 to 5 hours of direct sunlight per day.

Maintenance

Every plant, when fully established, requires a unique maintenance requirement. Apart from doing ordinary things like exposing your plants to the specific amounts of sunlight and water they need, certain plants demand extra care to be properly maintained. For example, you may need to prune some plants often to keep them in shape and prevent them from taking over extra space in your garden. The plants in this category are usually high-maintenance plants.

Hence, when deciding the kinds of plants to select for your needs, you must consider how much time you will likely have to keep your garden in order. I would recommend that you try to be as specific as possible because your answer will go a long way in helping you make the right decision. When you realize you have little time to spare for plant maintenance, you can easily go for low-maintenance plants that are guaranteed to make your work less. If it is the other way around, you can confidently pick up high-maintenance plants since you are assured you have enough time to take care of them.

It is also possible that though you have only a little time to spare for your garden tasks, you also have the resources to hire extra hands for the work. With that in mind, you can also assuredly select high-maintenance plants for your garden.

Colors

Who would agree with me that there is nothing more delightful and aesthetically pleasing than the way a perfectly designed garden tends to look when the flowers are in full bloom, showing off their bright colors? I bet a lot of you agree with me. However, not everyone is a fan of bright colors in their gardens. Some gardeners may want to have only green plants, which are less likely to attract insects. Notwithstanding the side you belong to, consider the colors of plants when deciding on the right kind of flowers, vegetables, and herbs to fill your garden space.

Pattern of Growth

Take a look at the plants around you, particularly the trees. You are likely first to notice that each has varying shapes and sizes. So, before you go ahead and select your plants, especially tree plants, you must endeavor to find out how big your preferred choices are likely to look in terms of shape and size when they are fully mature.

In case you are confused as to the importance of this side of the research, I want to remind you that right from your garden design phase, you have already reserved specific spaces for your plants. Thus, it would be wrong for your selected plant type to outgrow the area you have planted them in. It could alter the whole concept of your design.

Apart from the varying sizes, the roots of some plants tend to spread extensively. This could be a problem, especially if your planting area is quite close to your house, as the roots of most trees have a high potential of damaging the foundation of your home.

Seeds vs. Seedlings

Now that you understand the necessary factors to consider when choosing plants for your newly designed or redesigned garden space, you can either go to your local garden stores or online to purchase the most suitable plant types. But before you make your choices, we need to tackle one more dilemma you are likely to struggle with—do you purchase seeds or seedlings for any given plant type?

Once you know the appropriate plant types, whether vegetables, herbs, or flowers, that can grow well in your garden space, the next thing you have to decide is how you want to grow these plants. There are two available options you can decide to choose. First, you could decide to grow your plants right from the very beginning by sowing seeds. Or you could skip a few basic steps by using readily grown seedlings, also sometimes known as transplants.

Again, I must remind you that you are not allowed to make your decision based on impulse or assumptions. So how to best go about it? Each of the two options comes with its set of pros and cons. Hence, knowing and understanding the advantages and disadvantages will help you weigh out both options to determine the most suitable for your situation and needs.

Seeds—Pros

- **Affordability:** Not everybody has a surplus budget with which they can get all they want. Seeds are the more affordable option for growing your plants. Thus, if you are looking to save some extra change or are scared of spending too much on a new garden, you will be pleased to know that you can buy several seed packets for usually half the cost of one seedling.

- **More diverse choice:** "I don't have the luxury of time to search for my planting materials." Does that sound like you? Well, in the case of seeds, you will not have to look far or long because a large number of companies offer a wider array of seed varieties, including the most distinct ones. As such, you will not have to worry about the seeds of your selected garden plants being unavailable or in limited variety.

- **Experiencing the entire life cycle of growth:** My friend Caroline strongly believes that by growing her plants right from the seed, she gets to derive unique satisfaction comparable to nurturing and nourishing a newborn baby to the point of their youth. For gardeners like my friend Caroline, sowing seeds to grow their plants offers them the advantage of witnessing and participating in the entire cycle of their plants, from the point where it begins to germinate to the point where it grows into a sizable plant that is ripe for harvest.

Seeds—Cons

- **Less beginner-friendly:** One noticeable thing about seeds is that they are not the easiest option for beginners in the game of gardening. The process requires that you learn and gain a good amount of experience. So, with this option, you might try to figure out what works explicitly for the seeds and soil even after you have provided all the optimal conditions. You might want to ask yourself whether you are prepared to go through the trial-and-error process to gain the best experience of growing plants from seeds.

- **Longer growing period:** Beyond experience, growing your plants using seeds takes a lot of time and patience, two luxuries many of us may not be able to afford. To begin with, before the plant starts sprouting, you may have to wait about one to four weeks, depending on the plant type. After that, you will also have to wait a little longer for the plant to grow to the point where its roots are established, and only then can you transplant them to another flowerpot or garden bed. Going through these processes will require more work and patience.

- **Not all seeds will sprout:** Another major disadvantage of seed planting is that you cannot predict your outcome. Some seeds may not even emerge despite how cautious and meticulous you were in sowing and watering them. Many other factors you may be less able to control, like sufficient sunlight, adequate water, nutrient-rich soil, and having the weather and temperatures in mind, tend to influence such outcomes.

Seedlings—Pros

- **Offers a great head start:** Imagine having to build a house where the foundation had already been completed for you. It would make the work easier, right? Then, when you decide to go for seedlings, you are automatically jumping ahead of the basic steps in the plant's growth cycle. Once purchased, seedlings are usually ready to be planted in your garden beds immediately.
- **Enjoy a shorter growing season:** Using seedlings in regions where the growing season is relatively short is bliss! This is because it gives you an edge where you can plant quickly enough to maximize the warm weather and have more sunlight exposure.

- **Easier to keep alive:** When you buy healthy transplants from the closest local nursery to your garden, you will not have to worry about unpredictable results. Since the nursery homes are located in the same region as the one you live in, you have more assurance that the varieties you choose will also do well in your garden.

Seedlings—Cons

- **More Expensive:** Buying seedlings costs much more than buying seed packets, and the gap in their costs is explainable. Remember what we said about enjoying a head start with seedlings? Well, we cannot ignore the fact that someone had to spend some time caring for and tending those seeds to enable them to germinate well enough and be healthy to the point where you can buy them. So basically, you are paying more to supplement the prior services rendered.
- **Limited Choice:** While discussing the pros of using seeds for your plants, we explained that seeds are usually available in wider varieties. However, the same cannot be said for seedlings. In most cases, you may find out that your local nurseries sell plant varieties that locals commonly use. These varieties also tend to grow well based on the area's climate. As such, if you are looking for heirloom or uncommon plant varieties, you will likely not find such seedlings very easily.

Apart from the pros and cons we have just identified, you must also consider the specific kind of plants you selected in the first place and the region you live in when deciding if you want your plants to grow directly from seeds or seedlings. This consideration is even more critical in the case of seeds, and I will tell you why.

While some plants like beets, carrots, or lettuce typically do better when grown directly from seed, other long-season vegetable plants like tomatoes, peppers, and even eggplants may not fare well if grown from seeds, especially in regions with short-growing seasons. In such circumstances, your best option will be to purchase seedlings from your local nursery. Or better still, sow the seeds of these long-season plants and allow them to germinate indoors for a few weeks before the commencement of the planting season.

I have learned from my experience both as a gardener and garden designer that it is best to mix and match the two methods through the different seasons. But, how is that even possible? Remember I said earlier that every season is different and each comes with a new learning experience for you; thus, before the start of every planting season, you should try to look out for the factors that will help guide you on the best ways to make the most sense for your garden. For instance, it could be that in your first year as a gardener, you had extra gardening time because you were on vacation from work. For that reason, you opted for seeds to grow most of your plants. But as you proceed to the next season, you may not have as much free time. Automatically, you realize that your best option will be to get a jump start by purchasing seedlings.

One thing I love about this stage of post-design is that it is pretty straightforward. All you have to do is consider the factors we identified and observe as you proceed with your decisions. Now, this does not mean that you will not make mistakes. If there is one thing I have come to learn in the last few years, it is the fact that the best gardeners are those who make lots of mistakes but ultimately learn from every mistake!

Like I said earlier, every season will come with its own lessons, so observe thoroughly and consider the factors we discussed as you select the *right* plants that are best for your garden.

Chapter Summary

• The post-design stage involves selecting the right plants to fill your perfectly designed garden.

• Climate, maintenance, colors, and the plant's growth pattern are the four major factors to consider when trying to find the right plants for your garden.

• Start by listing out the types of plants you would prefer to grow in your garden, and then try to see if their sunlight and shade requirements are feasible with what is available in your particular plot.

• Your decisions on the right plant selection must also be based on how much time you will most likely have to spend keeping your garden in order.

• Plants have varying sizes and shapes. Thus you must ensure that the one you selected will not end up destroying the fence or foundation of your house.

• Once you have selected appropriate plants for your garden, you may decide to grow your plants right from the very beginning using seeds, or you could go for readily grown seedlings.

○ Seeds are very affordable and available in a diverse variety. Still, they are not the best choice for beginners due to the long growing period involved and the uncertainty of whether the seeds will even sprout at all.

○ With seedlings, you enjoy a head start and a shorter growing season. Also, it is easier to keep them alive because you are sure of their suitability for your environment. But unlike seeds, they are more expensive with limited availability.

NOTES

9

The 4 Essential Questions
Before You Start Landscaping

"Gardening is the purest of human pleasures."

Francis Bacon

So far, we have done quite a great job of getting the idea of your garden design project from your heart and mind and translating it onto paper. Basically, our main focus through the entire process of creating a sketch plan and then moving to a site survey, site inventory, site analysis, bubble plan, exploratory plan, and eventually your final design was to incorporate on paper most if not all of your garden design goals, wants and needs.

At the landscaping stage, you get to work and get your hands dirty as you try to physically recreate on your land what you have on paper.

But before you forge ahead into the world of landscaping, I will help you understand the essentials before you begin. So get your paper and pen because we are about to write down some details.

Question 1: Who?

The first essential question centers on you. Yes, you, the one with the big dream to create a perfectly designed garden. Okay, maybe I might need to rephrase more appropriately. The "who" question focuses on the circle of people that would be involved at any and every point of the landscaping project. Your job here is to find answers to questions like: who will participate in your garden project? Will your friends and family be available to help at some point? A typical answer might sound like this: "There are most likely going to be four people in my workforce, including myself, my boyfriend, and my two best friends."

Question 2: What?

The "what" question refers to the actual garden project itself; you are meant to provide details about the landscape project, such as what you want to achieve. Here you take inspiration from your garden goals to aid you—the "what" is about *what* you want to do to bring the garden to life.

The big question is what you plan to accomplish with this project. What goals do you want to achieve? Importantly, your answers must be as detailed as possible because, trust me, that is the best way to ensure you clearly define everything about the "what" element.

An example answer might sound like this: "I will be renovating the patio to make it ten by twelve feet and switching out the old woodworks for new ones." Remember our little exercise in Chapter 4 about setting garden goals? Now also ensure that your answers here are specific, measurable, and realistic.

Question 3: How?

Just as you have clearly defined the things you want to accomplish with your garden landscape project, you must also think deeply about how you will achieve those goals. Ask yourself, "Will I be doing all the work? Or will I be getting extra help? How many extra hands do I need to do the heavier lifting?"

An example answer might sound like this: "I want to adopt a DIY work style for my garden landscape. However, my boyfriend and two best friends will be available occasionally to help me. My boyfriend, Daniel, is very good at carpentry, so he will be helping mostly with the woodwork. However, my friend and I can handle the other areas quite well."

Now, the "how" element is not just about your workforce. It also involves the equipment and materials you need to complete the project. As such, you also have to figure out how much equipment you will need to accomplish each part of this landscape project and how you will get the necessary tools and materials.

It could be that all you need is a shovel, hoe, and wheelbarrow to turn your design ideas into landscape realities. On the other hand, you might have to bring in power equipment like tractors, side-cutters, etc. All of these are what you have to plan for as you figure out the "how."

Question 4: When?

It is extremely important that you analyze and plan out the amount of time you and perhaps your workforce will spend on accomplishing every task of your garden landscape design. Going about it this way will help you draw out a more accurate timeframe in which the project will be completed.

Remember, Rome was not built in a single day, so learn to take things one step at a time. There have been times when it took me over seven months to finish some of my projects. So ask yourself, "When will I do this or that task?" Sometimes you might realize that smaller tasks can easily be done and completed on weekends. During the weekdays, you focus more on the bigger and long-term tasks that could probably take months, depending on your time.

If you can successfully figure out and write down the details after answering these four essential questions we just discussed, you have gotten half of the landscaping job done! Sounds unbelievable, right? Having these well-defined details will give you a clear direction with which you can quickly and smoothly move through the landscaping process,s as you build and place each element in your final design plan.

Additional Budgeting and Planning Tips for Landscaping

Capital is an important element that you will definitely need to complete your garden project, whether it is for buying materials, hiring equipment, etc. Nonetheless, it is essential that you have a budget and a cost-saving plan so that you do not end up spending more than you should. Thus, as a final bonus to you, here are a few budgeting and cost-reduction tips that you can take advantage of when shopping for your landscaping materials and tools.

- **Research well:** Look at your garden wish list or your final design plan. Then try to list out all the materials you need to accomplish those goals. Once you have the list ready, do some research by walking around your local hardware stores, nurseries, and other landscape supply stores to find out the cost of each of those listed materials. When you finally add up the costs you have gathered, you can evaluate whether you are still within your initial capital budget or would have to readjust certain things to fit within your disposable capital.

- **Reuse and Recycle:** Remember in the final design sample, I reused the scattered boulders lying at the back of my sample property to decorate my backyard oasis? Well, you can do the same. Try to assess your available materials in your outdoor space and see if some of them can be reused, perhaps for a different purpose. You might discover that you do not have to buy some of the materials you listed earlier.

- **Buy materials in bulk or on sale:** Sometimes, gardeners often make the mistake of buying fewer units of essential material to save costs, but in most cases things work out differently for them. If you buy planting or landscaping materials in bulk, you can enjoy a more effective way of reducing costs. And even if you have extra left, you can always store it for the next time you will need it. On the other hand, you could also wait patiently to get some of your landscape and planting materials during sales in the off-season at the nurseries or landscape supply stores.

All in all, a new landscaping garden project tends to be quite costly, especially in terms of acquiring materials. However, suppose you can utilize the tips we just identified and approach the project smartly and thoughtfully. In that case, the design of your new garden will not cause any problems to your financial situation.

Chapter Summary

• There are four essential questions to ask—Who? What? How? When?—that you must figure out answers to before you proceed to the landscaping stage, where you will bring your final design plan to a reality.

○ The "who" question focuses on the number of people who will be involved at any and every point of the landscape project.

○ In analyzing the "what" question, you will have to provide adequate details about everything that concerns the actual landscape project and what you want to do to bring the project to realization.

○ The "how" question simply requires you to supply details of how you will accomplish the goals you identified in analyzing the "what" question.

○ Finally, answering the "when" question involves you planning out the amount of time you and perhaps your workforce will most likely spend on accomplishing each task of your garden landscape design.

• Since capital is an essential element that you will need for the completion of your garden project, it is also necessary that you have a budget and cost-saving plan.

○ Make sure to research the cost of each required material and add them up before you begin shopping.

○ Also, assess the available materials in your outdoor space and see if some can be reused, perhaps for a different purpose.

○ It would help if you also endeavored to buy planting or landscaping materials in bulk so that you get to enjoy a more effective way of reducing costs.

NOTES

Conclusion

We've made it to the very end! It was quite a journey, wasn't it? Writing this book has been one of the best decisions I have ever made in my life. Of course, this adventure was not easy, but you know what kept me going? The fact I believe in wonderful readers like you, willing to learn how you can achieve your dreams of creating the perfect garden!

In the introduction of this book, I made several promises, all of which I could fulfill until we had a complete house of knowledge with nine floors, or what you can call chapters! In the beginning, we started with the foundations, in which we discussed everything that should be considered before starting your garden design, from creating a garden wants and needs list that fits with your lifestyle to analyzing all the environmental factors (sunlight exposure, wind, soil types, insects and animals) and how it could influence your design.

As we climbed upwards towards the third and fourth floors, we analyzed the different garden styles you can choose as your concept design and how you can define your goals using the SMR formula. From this point, we settled down to begin the actual process of designing, which involves creating sketch

Conclusion

plans, a site survey, site inventory, site analysis, bubble plans, and exploratory plans. Eventually, we were able to create our final design plan. To ensure that we did not leave any loose ends, we went further to explore what the post-design stage involves and the essential factors to consider before one starts landscaping. As icing on the cake, I gave a few expert tips with which you can budget appropriately to save on costs as you begin your garden landscape.

You will hopefully agree that together we have erected a very high building of garden design knowledge. As such, you have all the necessary tools to make your dream of creating your perfect garden come to life. I must also emphasize that the knowledge and understanding you have gained from reading this book is more than enough proof that you can create your perfect garden design without incurring the kind of expense that may leave a giant dent in your bank account.

The most important rule is not to skip a step because each step is the foundation for the next step. And don't feel pressured! Remember, the best gardeners are those who make mistakes and learn from them. So take your time as you try to practice every step you have learned here. Most importantly, you never give up because your perfectly designed and personalized garden is just around the corner, if not already completed!

Before you go ahead and make your dream a reality, I'd like to ask you to please leave a review on Amazon if you enjoyed this book. I would also love it if you gave me feedback on your progress in our Facebook group called Garden design + gardening tips and tricks, which is filled with more than a thousand helpful gardeners who are eager to welcome you. I am itching to see what your garden will look like, and confident you will create beautiful and magical masterpieces. I cant wait to see you there!

LEAVE A ONE-CLICK REVIEW!

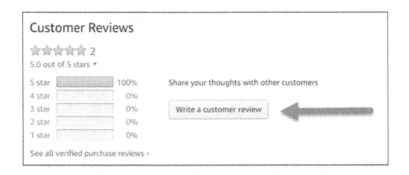

If you enjoyed reading our book and would like to share your opinion on it, please be so kind as to leave a review on Amazon. This will help our book stand out amongst the big competition!

Also by The Garden Architect

Ranked #1 in family activities

Want to start gardening with your kids?

Gardening For Kids is a book on how to create a beautiful garden with your children even if you have absolutely zero experience with gardening or have failed at gardening before! *Gardening For Kids* will act as your friendly guide and will show you step-by-step how to create a beautiful garden. So, you and your kids have nothing to worry about!

In this list of gardening mistakes, you MUST avoid, you will learn:

- Thirteen of the most commonly made mistakes beginner gardeners make without realizing it.
- The secret to unlimited amounts of gardening knowledge. Without having to learn a damn thing!
- How to be part of our Facebook community filled with friendly and supportive gardeners.

Scan the QR code below with your mobile device to receive your **FREE BONUS GIFT!**
Or go to www.thegardenarchitectbooks.com.

References

Allen, Monique. "The Importance of Understanding Available Sun for Your Garden." The Garden Continuum, August 2019. < https://www.thegardencontinuum.com/blog/the-importance-of-understanding-available-sun-for-your-garden >, retrieved August 2022.

Association of Professional Landscape Designers, California Chapter. "Landscape Design Checklist." < http://apldca.org/what-is-landscape-design/landscape-design-checklist >, retrieved August 2022.

Ainapure, H. "3 Basic Styles Of Gardening." Ugaoo website, 2019. <https://www.ugaoo.com/knowledge-center/3-basic-styles-of-gardening>, retrieved August 2022.

"Find Out Your Soil Type." BBC Gardeners' World Magazine, May 11, 2019. <https://www.gardenersworld.com/plants/find-out-your-soil-type>, retrieved August 2022.

Berle, D. "Drawing a Landscape Plan - Site Analysis." University of Georgia Extension website. <https://extension.uga.edu/publications/detail.html?number=C1032-4&title=Drawing%20a%20Landscape%20Plan%20-%20Site%20Analysis>, retrieved August 2022.

Campbell, A. "How To Choose a Garden Style – 12 Beautiful Garden Design Ideas." The Middle-Sized Garden, February 7, 2021. <https://www.themiddlesizedgarden.co.uk/how-choose-garden-style-11-beautiful-garden-design-ideas>, retrieved August 2022.

Chen, X. "An Analysis of Climate Impact on Landscape Design." *Atmospheric and Climate Sciences,* 6:3, July 2016. < https://www.scirp.org/journal/paperinformation.aspx?paperid=68916>, retrieved August 2022.

"Bubble diagrams in Landscape Design." ConceptDraw application website. <https://www.conceptdraw.com/How-To-Guide/bubble-diagrams-landscape>, retrieved August 2022.

David, Lauren. "What's the Difference Between Sowing Seeds and Planting Starts?" Allrecipes, March 30, 2021. <https://www.allrecipes.com/article/difference-between-sowing-seeds-and-planting-starts>, retrieved August 2022.

"Complete the Site Survey for your Garden Design." Design Gardens, 2013. <http://www.design-gardens.com/site-survey.html>, retrieved August 2022.

Duford, Mary Jane. "How to Set Gardening Goals You'll Actually Achieve." Home for the Harvest, July 31, 2022. <https://www.homefortheharvest.com/how-to-set-gardening-goals>, retrieved August 2022.

Fedele, Amy. "Garden Styles: What Type is Right For You?" Pretty Purple Door, December 8, 2021. <https://www.prettypurpledoor.com/garden-styles>, retrieved August 2022.

"Drawing the Garden Plan." Garden Design Exposed! <https://www.gardendesignexposed.com/garden_plan.html>, retrieved August 2022.

Hansen, G. And Alvarez, A. "Landscape Design: Analyzing Site Conditions." University of Florida Extension. <https://edis.ifas.ufl.edu/publication/EP426>, retrieved August 2022.

Holmes, Kier. "Expert Advice: A Landscape Designer Shares Her Best Money-Saving Tips." Gardenista, March 17, 2020. <https://www.gardenista.com/posts/expert-advice-landscape-designer-shares-best-money-saving-tips>, retrieved August 2022.

Horspool, S. "Weather and Environmental Factors in Green Landscape Design." Dengarden, February 21, 2022. <https://dengarden.com/gardening/Climate-Factors-in-Landscape-Design>, retrieved August 2022.

Iannotti, M. "Vegetable Seeds or Seedlings? Find Out Which Is Best for Your Garden." The Spruce, October 20, 2021. <https://www.thespruce.com/vegetable-garden-seeds-or-seedlings-1403412>, retrieved August 2022.

Kristin G. "Be SMART with Gardening Goals!" University of Kentucky College of Agriculture, Food and Environment. <https://warrencountyagriculture.com/tag/being-smart-with-garden-goals>, retrieved August 2022.

"Site Analysis." Landscape America. <http://www.landscape-america.com/landscapes/design/site.html>, retrieved August 2022.

"Site Inventory and Analysis for Water Wise Landscapes." Water Conservation for Lawn and Landscape website, July 29, 2019. <https://landscape-water-conservation.extension.org/site-inventory-and-analysis-for-water-wise-landscapes>, retrieved August 2022.

Leavitt, Laura. "How to Protect Your Garden from Wind." Dave's Garden, July 5, 2018. <https://davesgarden.com/guides/articles/how-to-protect-your-garden-from-wind>, retrieved August 2022.

Mathews, R. (2019). How To Survey Your Garden And Draw A Scale Plan ~ The Critical First Stage to a Great Garden.

"A Beginner's Guide to DIY Landscaping In 2021" [video file]. Yard Coach YouTube channel. <https://youtu.be/J3Hatw1O-vQ>, retrieved August 2022.

Neverman, Laurie. "Too Much Rain in the Garden – Managing Wet Dirt and Waterlogged Plants." Common Sense Home, July 1, 2017. < https://commonsensehome.com/too-much-rain >, retrieved August 2022.

Designing Your Garden: Bubble Diagrams." Paper Garden Workshop. < https://www.papergardenworkshop.com/blog/designing-your-garden-bubble-diagrams >, retrieved August 2022.

Robert, P. "Landscape Design: Learn to Create Your Own Garden Design" [video files]. Garden Fundamentals YouTube channel, January 2021. Part 2: < https://youtu.be/3NjHoPg6ES8 >. Part 3: < https://youtu.be/Dy4cVq9yFXI >. Part 5: < https://youtu.be/Y_VG5E56ExQ >. Part 6: < https://youtu.be/6agXwD2-DSs >. Part 7: < https://youtu.be/FoGHszxmc2c >. All retrieved August 2022.

Saunders, Manu. "Your Garden Is an Ecosystem, And It Needs Looking After." The Conversation, September 27, 2016. <https://theconversation.com/amp/birds-bees-and-bugs-your-garden-is-an-ecosystem-and-it-needs-looking-after-65226>, retrieved August 2022.

Toscano, Kim. "A Gardener's Guide to Sun Exposure." Southern Living Plant Collection, April 1, 2022. <https://southernlivingplants.com/planting-care/a-gardeners-guide-to-sun-exposure>, retrieved August 2022.

Vanheems, Benedict. "10 Things I Wish I'd Known Before Starting a Vegetable Garden." GrowVeg website, February 8, 2019. <https://www.growveg.com/guides/10-things-i-wish-id-known-before-starting-a-vegetable-garden>, retrieved August 2022.

Van Leeuwen, Hendrik. "Plant Selection: Top 6 Things to Consider for Your Garden." Van Leeuwen Green, May 2016. <https://www.vanleeuwengreen.com/blog/plant-selection-top-6-things-consider-garden>, retrieved August 2022.

Yuliya, B. "Garden Design: How to Design a Garden" [video file]. Y Garden YouTube channel, February 2020. Part 1: < https://youtu.be/wRGzNzLiSjk >. Part 2: < https://youtu.be/rpV5KtqTCGI >. Both retrieved August 2022.

Made in the USA
Las Vegas, NV
11 October 2023

78947585R00094